SIGNS OF THE COMING CHRIST

A SCRIPTURAL REFERENCE GUIDE FOR END TIMES PROPHECY

R. Scott Sykes, MD

XULON PRESS

D0681528

CONTENTS

ONE

AN INTRODUCTION TO PROPHECY

Matthew 24:4-8: Jesus answered: "Watch out that no one deceives you. For many will come in my name, claiming, 'I am the Christ', and will deceive many. You will hear of war and rumors of war, but see to it that you are not alarmed. Such things must happen, but the end is still to come. Nation will rise against nation, and kingdom against kingdom. There will be famines and earthquakes in various places. All these things are the beginnings of birth pains."

As I approached the break room of my office building the morning of September 11, 2001, I noticed the room was unusually crowded. Everyone seemed to be watching the small television in the corner of the room. Some of the people were crying softly, while others just stared in disbelief. As I turned to the television, I too stared in disbelief just as the second plane hit the building. Stunned silence quickly evolved into a palpable sense of fear. We were under attack and no one knew what might happen next. This couldn't be happening – the unthinkable had actually occurred. Not since Pearl Harbor had the U.S. homeland been attacked like this. Moments later the building was empty; we all decided to go back to our families and watch the news from home.

Many of my friends began to call me as soon as I

returned home. They knew that biblical prophecy was a passion of mine, and that I had distinct opinions regarding many of the current events taking place in the world. Previous discussions on the topic of future prophecy had been met with both skepticism and disbelief, but not this time. Most of my friends and colleagues were concerned about the immediate future and they wanted any information pertinent to these events. The morning of September 11 was simply too big and too frightening for conventional answers or the usual rhetoric. Many people wanted to know what the Bible had to say as no other sources seemed to have the answers. The bewilderment, confusion and lack of information defined everyone from the White House to the common citizen. With no place else to look for answers; many flocked to the local churches seeking a sense of reassurance. Prophecy was being discussed, not only in the churches but also in the media, as well-known prophecy scholars were being interviewed frequently. I wondered how long this interest in Bible prophecy would last.

A New World

The constant threat of terrorism has changed our lives in many ways; certainly more than almost anyone could have imagined. As America and other countries fight this war across the globe, our freedoms have increasingly eroded. The war on terror necessitated an array of additional security measures, all of which impose to some degree, an invasion of individual privacy and rights. A one-world governmental policy or at least a unified approach among industrialized countries has been suggested as a method of combating terrorism. At the same time, we worry about the threat of extremist groups triggering nuclear detonations or "dirty bombs" in one or more of our cities with the resulting impact on the economy. We watch the news and see the many rumors of war, potentially involving weapons of mass destruction: North Korea threatening to invade South Korea, China threatening Taiwan, Israel warning that they will destroy the nuclear facility in Iran with Iran threatening a massive retaliation, India and Pakistan engaging in nuclear brinkmanship, North Korea implying that their nuclear missiles can be launched and reach the U.S. mainland, the constant rumor of the U.S. expanding the war against terror and, of course the Islamic terror groups, who threaten all industrialized countries on a daily basis. Now that the unthinkable had actually occurred, these other ongoing threats seemed closer to becoming a reality and seemed more imminent.

Many people today find themselves living with a sense of concern or apprehension, wondering what the future will bring. Do the terrorists possess weapons of mass destruction, perhaps even nuclear capability? If so, will they be used? How will the "attacked" countries respond? Will further war develop? Will a massive, coordinated attack take place as threatened? Will freedoms now enjoyed become obsolete, as industrialized countries impose even greater restrictions on their citizens, for the purpose of fighting terrorism? These are just a few of the questions that are now discussed casually; questions that would have been considered shocking for past generations. The type of world that our children will inherit has become an increasingly ominous concern. What once seemed like a certain, predictable future has now become questionable, uncertain and unpredictable.

Prophecy for Today

Amazingly, future world events have been described in

great detail, and recorded in the Bible by ancient Prophets - Prophets who have yet to be wrong. Hundreds of their prophecies have already been fulfilled and history tells us that these events occurred in the exact manner as they had been predicted. These same Prophets gave considerable attention to this final period; a dramatic time described as being unlike any other period ever experienced on earth. Not only are these events destined for the future, but there are compelling reasons to believe that these prophetic writings are applicable to our current age. World events today are unfolding in the precise manner that the Prophets recorded – events that will ultimately precede the Second Coming of Jesus Christ. Biblical prophecy contains this information with a comprehensive yet detailed view of the future.

I would compare the study of Bible prophecy to uncovering new scientific discoveries; a process that comes with unexpected surprises and great anticipation of future information. For prophecy watchers, significant world events are occurring at a breathtaking pace; events that not only confirm the undeniable accuracy of prophecy, but also give ample proof of the existence of a real and living God. There is simply no other way to explain the accurate fulfillment of hundreds of specific predictions made over a period of thousands of years. Even the Bible itself declares that the evidence of fulfilled prophecy gives undeniable proof of God's role in prophecy: Isaiah 42:9, *"See, the former things have taken place, and new things I declare; before they spring into being I announce them to you."* 2 Peter 1:20-21 repeats the same message: *"Above all, you must understand that no prophecy of Scripture came about by the prophet's own interpretation. For prophecy never had its origin in the will of man, but men spoke from God."* Thus, we have at our disposal, an existing "database" of previously fulfilled prophecy that absolutely compels us to seriously consider all remaining biblical predictions as they pertain to our future.

Understanding prophecy actually changed the way I viewed and studied the entire Bible. Rather than a dated and seemingly uninteresting book, it became a living, breathing document, containing specific application to life on earth today. I couldn't help but realize the awesome nature of an omnipotent God, who has given us ample information regarding our personal future and the future of this planet. I could also see current prophecy fulfillment occurring exactly as predicted in the Bible simply by reading and watching the daily news. The more I learned about the multitude of fascinating predictions and fulfillments from these Old Testament writings, the more I desired even greater understanding, which subsequently led to further study and research. The realization struck that I was reading not only about my immediate future, but how huge, world events would continue to unfold in the coming years.

The various "signs" for which we have been instructed to watch, are becoming realities on a daily basis. Significant, prophetic events have been occurring at a staggering rate, thus confirming what we already know about previously fulfilled prophecies: future prophecies will unfold in a literal manner, just as they have been written. Over 2,500 years ago it was predicted that Jerusalem, in the latter days, would become the focus of the world's attention (Zechariah 12:3), just as it is today. This attention began when Israel regained the city during the war of 1967. Following this time, the world has witnessed the conflict escalate into the violence we see today. The very fact that the status of a small, seemingly insignificant city such as Jerusalem would become a world-wide concern after almost 2,000 years of insignificance, gives us yet another fascinating literal fulfillment of prophecy.

Perhaps even more significant however, was the prophecy from Ezekiel that foretold the regathering of the nation of Israel, after almost 2,000 years of exile. Despite having been scattered throughout the world (also predicted by Ezekiel) for this 2,000 year period, Israel was reborn as a nation, virtually overnight in 1948. No other nation has ever ceased to exist, particularly over a period of centuries, and returned become a country. Certainly, a nation has never been formed "in a day", yet that is exactly what happened on May 15, 1948. The prophecies of Isaiah (Isaiah 66:8) and Ezekiel (Ezekiel 36, 37) were fulfilled precisely as written on this miraculous date in history. This dramatic fulfillment of biblical prophecy also seems to have signaled the beginning of this last remaining cluster of prophecy. Before this significant date in 1948, there had been a long period of prophetic silence, but since that date, prophecy has been occurring at a phenomenal rate. It seems that this formal rebirth of the nation of Israel in some way signaled the beginning of the end of this age.

Prophecy is obviously very important in our understanding of the Bible, simply considering that over 25% of all scriptures are devoted to prophecy. Can you imagine trying to read and understand a novel if one-fourth of the book was deleted and the deletion included the final chapter? It is also abundantly clear from the scriptures that the "last generation" should understand that they are indeed living in the final age. Jesus made this point on multiple occasions. There are specific instructions intended for living in the final generation. Jesus, Paul, Peter and John all devoted considerable time to the subject and gave us detailed information. Jesus consistently told us to watch and be prepared for His return. He even gave us specific signs for which to watch. Jesus devoted considerable time and attention to prophecy during His final moments on earth.

With a detailed understanding of the prophetic writings pertinent for our age, it became very clear to me that we are without a doubt, living in the last generation – the last generation that Jesus described in His discussion at the Mount of Olives only two days before His arrest. The urgency with which Jesus discussed end time prophecy during His last days on earth, struck me as a glaring reminder of its vast importance. In simple terms, if it is important to Jesus, it should be important to me.

Prophecy Data: A Scientific Approach

Because of my medical and research training, I approached the study of prophecy in a very objective, analytical manner. As a physician originally schooled at an academic center, subsequently followed by 20 years of conducting medical research, I decided to approach the study of prophecy in the same way that I had learned to collect and analyze research data. There are basic "rules" of conducting scientific research which have been established and followed throughout the last century. Medical advances and breakthrough treatment modalities must strictly follow these rules or guidelines in order to gain acceptance in the medical community. Otherwise, false, erroneous conclusions could be determined from the data resulting in patients receiving inappropriate treatment. The scientific/medical community strictly adheres to these principles in order to avoid incorrect conclusions.

The first principle in conducting scientific research involves the elimination of any preconceived thoughts or ideas which may influence how the data are analyzed. This is the only way to appropriately analyze data, as preconceived ideas create bias which typically leads to false conclusions. One of the most important aspects of conducting clinical research is to remove any potential for bias. The study of Bible prophecy "data" is no different. Fortunately, early in my process of studying prophecy my relative lack of knowledge was a blessing; I had no preconceived "answers" regarding the topic of prophecy interpretation. In fact, I was unaware of the various "arguments" or the passion involved within the Church regarding the differences in opinion.

The second step in this analytical approach was to collect and study as much "data" as possible; in this case a collection of all applicable scripture, related literature and commentary books relating to end times prophecy. This process included reading as many differing opinions as possible, in an effort to view as much data as possible before arriving at my own conclusions. You might say that I was looking to establish the "preponderance" of evidence based on all of the cumulative facts. I wasn't concerned with the specific outcome of this research – I just wanted it to be scripturally correct and accurate. I was searching for the truth.

The next step in this research-based approach involved the issue of reading prophecy as literal writings to be understood exactly as written versus the method of reading prophecy as "allegorical" or symbolic writings. By the symbolic approach, one must look for deeper, underlying messages which may give different meanings from the actual words themselves. I learned that virtually every disagreement in interpreting prophecy is ultimately based upon the difference in the "literal" versus the "allegorical" method of interpretation. It was obvious to me that this topic could not be taken lightly; determination of this most basic fundamental approach to prophecy could lead to very different paths in understanding.

The first method I used in this effort of determining whether I would adopt a literal approach or a symbolic approach seemed obvious, particularly when using a scientific approach. I simply reviewed the Old Testament prophecies which have already been fulfilled, in order to see specifically how they were fulfilled. Much to my utter amazement, I saw that the Old Testament prophecies had been fulfilled in a very literal manner. I didn't have to create symbolism – the words explained the prophecies just as they were written. Any careful analysis of Old Testament prophecies will reveal a staggering number of specific, precise prophecies concerning not only entire nations and their people, but specific events recorded in history. Each of these predictions has been fulfilled with an amazing degree of accuracy and precision.

I then studied those prophecies revealing detailed information about the birth, life, death and resurrection of Jesus, and again, discovered that these were fulfilled literally and specifically. According to biblical scholar Grant Jeffery, there are 48 detailed, specific prophecies centered on Jesus – all fulfilled in a literal manner (1). Just taking 17 of these literal prophecies and estimating the random probability of these events happening by *chance* is well over 1 in 480 billion x 1 trillion (2).

It was also easy to see that whenever Jesus referenced the Old Testament prophecies, he did so in a literal way. A brief review of the four Gospels (Matthew, Mark, Luke and John) will quickly reveal how often Jesus referred to prophecy in His daily conversations. He answered questions by quoting prophecy scriptures, He referenced the fulfillment of prophecy as it occurred, and He instructed His disciples to read and understand prophecy. Clearly, prophecy was an important part of Jesus' teachings. Importantly, Jesus referred to all prophecy, both past and future in a literal way. It also made sense that Jesus would do so, because any type of symbolism is highly variable and dependent upon the individual reader, yet a literal fulfillment can be read the same way by everyone.

There were other concerns regarding the use of symbolism. If future prophecy is to be read symbolically with the use of confusing allegory, as some suggest, why would God make this future prophecy so vastly different from past prophecy? In simple terms, if past prophecy was fulfilled literally, why wouldn't future prophecy reach fulfillment in the same literal manner? With the clear understanding that prophecy has great importance to God – why would he play games with the subject by hiding the truth in confusing and variable allegories? Why would scriptures of such importance be based upon whether I am able to guess their meaning correctly? In addition, my "research" determined that different scholars who attempted to allegorize the prophecies had a great deal of variation on their different "interpretations". These differences in opinion, often seen with the symbolic approach, contrasted distinctively to the opinions given by the evangelical authors who had little variance in their literal interpretations. The literal method of interpreting prophecy scripture was much more consistent among the various prophecy scholars. Additionally, the authors who have taken a literal approach have been highly consistent in their views over a 40-50 year period.

Once I determined that the literal approach made the most sense, I came upon another big discovery - reading prophecy is not that difficult. It's actually relatively straightforward and typically unambiguous, unlike what I had been told throughout my Christian life. This understanding led to rather obvious questions confirming this point: "Who is the Bible written for, a handful of professors at a School of Theology? Or, did God intend the Bible (and prophecy) to be read by everyone?" It was apparent to me, that a literal interpretation is something that anyone can read and understand, regardless of credentials or academic accomplishments. Predictably, using such a literal interpretation makes perfect sense as well and it all fits together like an intricate puzzle, with no missing pieces.

Prophecy Data: Organizing the Information

This brings us to the primary purpose of this book. After studying the various scriptures from prophecy for approximately 20 years, I became disappointed that I was unable to consistently reference the applicable scriptures whenever I tried to engage the topic with someone. Despite having read various books and the pertinent scriptures countless times, I still found myself floundering with quick recall of the scriptural references. This made it hard to communicate truths when engaging in these discussions. With this realization, I then decided to put together an outline for my own purposes – an outline that would contain all of the scriptural references pertinent to the prophecies as they apply to current events. This was very useful, however with the outline containing only references I was still spending considerable time looking up the scripture in my study Bibles. By adding the actual scriptures to the outline, considerable time and effort was saved during the study of end time prophecies. At this point I determined that using this same approach in a book format may help others study, understand and learn the prophetic writings as they apply to our generation.

I also find it easier to learn by visually bolding or highlighting the most important aspects of the scripture, as your eyes are quickly led to the key phrase or the key segment of a given scripture. Thus, the reader will find smaller "segments" of text with a frequent use of italics and bolded print. Additionally, I have quoted as much pertinent scripture as possible, thus preventing the readers from having to stop and locate the passages from their Bibles. Tangential scriptures and additional scriptures of interest have been referenced as well.

My desire is to weigh the balance of scripture and commentary towards less commentary and more scripture. The direct words from the prophets themselves often require little commentary. Ultimately, the main goal is simply a consolidation of the various scriptures which apply to a given topic. One will also find several areas of redundancy. The scriptures offer redundancy with many important "sections" of prophecy. Rather than detail such information only once, the reader may find the same information repeated several times throughout this book. This repetition aids in learning the scriptures, plus the areas of repetition may allow the reader to see the consistency of prophetic themes as they appear in different parts of the Bible. I hope this approach is helpful. If there is a problem with prophecy it's not a lack of prophecy; the problem arises from the fact that there is so much prophecy, particularly prophecy regarding the final generation. Hopefully the following chapters will serve as a useful aid in the study of prophecy scriptures as we watch these world events unfold exactly as predicted in the scriptures.

CHAPTER ONE NOTES

1. Grant R. Jeffery. Triumphant Return. The Coming Kingdom of God (Frontier Research Publications, Inc. 2001).

2. Grant R. Jeffrey. The Signature of God. (Thomas Nelson Inc. - W Publishing Group, 1998).

TWO

AN OVERVIEW OF THE FUTURE

2 Peter 1:19-21: And we have the word of the prophets made more certain, and you will do well to pay attention to it, as to a light shining in a dark place, until the day dawns and the morning star rises in your hearts. Above all, understand that no prophecy came about by the prophet's own interpretation. For prophecy never had its origin in the will of man, but men spoke from God, as they were carried along by the Holy Spirit.

World events today are taking a more and more ominous tone every day. The threat from terrorism has escalated to the point that virtually every government is being forced to determine how they will react to potential epic disasters. Nuclear technology has escaped the tight circle which had been created by the old Soviet Union and the United States. Now, multiple countries possess nuclear technology and the missiles which can carry these destructive weapons around the planet. This technology has also escaped into the hands of terrorist groups who are feverishly working to obtain the necessary materials, so that they can use these weapons for their purposes. Rumors circulate that so-called "suitcase nuclear weapons", which describe small nuclear weapons designed to fit within a suitcase, have been stolen from Russia and are now in the hands of extremist groups. Biological and chemical weapons are also stored in vast amounts in many countries who share the same basic ideology with these terrorist groups.

At the same time, we see highly unusual weather patterns resulting in drought in some areas of the world yet producing hurricanes and flooding in other areas. Earthquakes have dramatically increased in frequency and severity, plus, they have been occurring in many "diverse" places. Deaths from famine have grown as refugee camps have become the norm in many regions following the regional conflicts and as a combination of floods and drought have diminished food production in much of the world. War has been a constant throughout the world during the past century, particularly considering the two world wars of the twentieth century.

Over the course of the last decade, there has been constant discussion of real and potential war, including the wars in Iraq and Afghanistan, the tensions between China and Taiwan, the threat of nuclear war between India and Pakistan, the civil wars that have ravished Africa, North Korea's constant threat of nuclear war and of invading South Korea, the ongoing Middle-East conflict, the "rumor" of Syria harboring terrorists and weapons of mass destruction, Israel threatening to destroy Iran's nuclear facilities, and the constant threat of terrorism facing industrialized nations, just to name a few. The world witnessed a 40 year rumor of war during the cold war era between the U.S. and Soviet Union.

Yet despite the world wars and increasing threats of terrorism, the events of September 11, 2001 changed the world dramatically. Most people today seem to feel that the world is moving towards some type of climax. It is hard to imagine that the progression of these current events will reverse course or that the world will suddenly become a peaceful, harmonious place. Instead, these ominous events seem to be increasing in speed and magnitude. However, the good news is that almost everything we see in the world today is described in the words of prophecy contained within the Bible. The final stages of the world's events have been described in great detail by the prophets; the same prophets who have been 100% accurate in their earlier predictions. All we have to do is read their words in order to understand how multiple current events are coming together just as foretold thousands of years ago.

We can trust the prophecies contained within the Bible, simply because of the vast number of prophecies which have already been fulfilled in a literal manner. The final, remaining cluster of prophecies are centered on concluding world events; events which will occur just before the Second Coming of Christ. The Bible devotes an enormous amount of text to this issue and these prophetic writings are of obvious importance. Jesus spent considerable time discussing these events, as did John, Paul and Peter. To know the future, all you have to do is simply read Bible prophecy. Because we appear to be living in the last generation as described by the prophets, it is tremendously important to understand and watch for the "signs" which have been described throughout the Bible.

A literal interpretation of future prophecy gives significant and detailed information for our generation. The beginning of this last cluster of prophecy really started in 1948, with the miraculous regathering of the nation of Israel. This prophecy was given in Ezekiel 36 and 37, where the scattering of the people of Israel is detailed, "I dispersed them among the nations and they were scattered through the countries" (Ezek. 36:19). This destruction of Jerusalem by the Romans in 70 A.D. marked the beginning of this "scattering" of Israel's people. Beginning with Ezekiel 36:24 and throughout Ezekiel 37, the regathering of the nation of Israel is described. The formation of Israel as a nation in 1948 was unprecedented. Never before has an entire nation and culture been destroyed and dispersed throughout the world, and then regathered as a nation thousands of years later.

Prophecy tells us that just before the Second Coming of Christ, there will be a revival or a regrouping of the ancient Roman Empire (Daniel 2, 7 and 9), which existed at the time of Christ. The book of Daniel gives great detail regarding this last world government and how it will encompass the entire world. Currently we have witnessed first stages of this empire, in the form of the expanding European Union. With the 25 countries currently forming the EU, one can easily compare the geographical cluster of these nations with a map of the first Roman Empire and the resemblance between the two is uncanny. Even as recently as 20 years ago, the formation of such a "United States of Europe" was unthinkable, yet just as prophecy foretold, it has happened.

Following this miraculous rebirth of Israel as a nation, and the reunification of the old Roman Empire, prophecy tells us that a single individual will emerge as a world leader. However, before his public "coming out" (signified by his brokering of a peace plan in the Middle-East), the Church – the body of believers in Christ - will experience a rather dramatic event: the Rapture (1 Corinthians 15:42-55; 1 Thessalonians 4:15-17; 2 Thessalonians 2:6-8).

The Rapture of the Church is described as two-step process. First the "dead in Christ" (believers who have died) will rise first, receiving "incorruptible" bodies, or "glorified bodies". This process involves the souls of these believers, reuniting with new, glorified bodies which can then experience eternity in the heavenly realm. Immediately after this, in a "twinkling of the eye", the living believers will be changed into their glorified, heavenly bodies and will meet Christ "in the air". In an instant, the body of believers, known as the Church, will literally disappear from earth in a manner similar to Elijah's Rapture (2 Kings 2:11-12). Christ will then take His Church to his Father's house in order to be with Him forever (John 14:1-3).

At an unknown time after the Rapture (presumably soon afterwards), this world figure will formally emerge by his "confirming" an apparent peace plan for Israel and her neighbors in the Middle-East (Daniel 8:25, 9:27; 1 Thessalonians 5:3). This individual is called by many names, but most commonly he is referred to as "the Antichrist" (1 John 4:3). He will emerge from one of the countries forming the European Union, because the EU represents a revival of the old Roman Empire. This individual, in concert with "ten kings" (Daniel 7:24; Revelation 17:12-13), will rule over the entire world (Revelation 13:7). He will initially appear to be a peace-maker, however the peace will be short-lived and war will break out (Revelation 6:4; Daniel 8:25). This peace "covenant" signals the beginning of a seven year period called the "Tribulation", and also serves as a "red-flag" warning that he is indeed the figure known biblically as the Antichrist (2 Thessalonians 2:6-8; Daniel 9:27).

This seven year Tribulation is described in great detail in Revelation 6-18, and will consist of 21 separate "judgments" cast upon earth. These judgments will ultimately destroy most of the earth, will kill the majority of humans on earth and will be a time like none other in the history of the world (Revelation 6-18; Matthew 24:21). This period will be so destructive, that if Jesus does not appear (Second Coming) in order to end it, there will be no survivors (Matthew 24:22). During this time, however, many will come to accept Christ (Revelation 7:9).

The Tribulation will consist of a final period on earth – a period in which every living person will have an opportunity to choose between either Christ or the Antichrist. This final period on earth as we know it will represent a last chance for individuals to make their eternal choice, and thus determine their eternal destiny. God will make His presence abundantly clear during the Tribulation. Those who reject Him will do so despite the abundance of evidence given to them; evidence which will serve to confirm the presence of God. Consistent with God's will for man throughout history, man will again have complete freedom to decide how they will spend eternity – in the presence of God or in the absence of God. God will not dictate man's chosen fate. He leaves that decision for each individual.

At the mid-point of this seven year Tribulation, the Antichrist will appear in the re-built Jewish Temple in Jerusalem, and he will proclaim himself as God. This single event will serve as the signal that the period of intense persecution and severe judgments has begun (Daniel 7:25; 9:27; Matthew 24:15; Revelation 13:5-7). The people living in Jerusalem are told to flee immediately when this happens, as persecution will reach epic levels. The Antichrist will force people to worship him or else face death (Daniel 7:25; Revelation 13:7, 13:15). He will rule over a one-world government with a unified finance system based upon the "Mark of the Beast", which is another way people will declare their allegiance to the Antichrist. This mark, which is described as something individuals receive on their right hand or forehead will be necessary in order to buy or sell, or engage in any financial transaction (Revelation 13:16-17). The Antichrist will also perform seemingly miraculous signs and he will be given the power to deceive many (Daniel 8:25; Revelation 13:14).

At the very end of the Tribulation, the Second Coming of Christ will occur (Daniel 2:44; 7:26-27; Revelation 19:11-16). The events of the Second Coming are described in Revelation, Matthew and Zechariah. The earth will darken; there will be a "sign" in the sky which will presumably draw the attention of survivors of the Tribulation to that special place in the sky. At this point the heavens will open, and all inhabitants of the earth will see Christ returning in His glory and splendor. Then the Christ will strike down the Antichrist and the False Prophet, and the battles of "Armageddon" will end with Christ's ultimate victory (Revelation 19:19-21). Following these significant events, Christ will reign on earth for 1,000 years, in a peaceful, renewed earth (Revelation 20; Isaiah 2:4, 11:6, 11:9, and 65:20). The earth will be populated by those who survived the Tribulation and accepted the truth about Christ. At the very end of this 1,000 year period, Satan will be "released" and he will stage one final rebellion. This rebellion will consist of Satan "deceiving the nations" and gathering those deceived for the purpose of battle. They will surround Jerusalem, but before battle, this gathering will be ended in a supernatural manner directly by the hand of God (Revelation 20). Satan will be removed forever. The next events described include the creation of a "new heaven and a new earth" which will allow man to live with "the Lord God Almighty and the Lamb" forever (Revelation 21 and 22). The book of Revelation describes the Holy City, New Jerusalem throughout these final two chapters.

The description given above is a very broad overview of the events which will take place in the future. There are many additional details regarding these prophecies; details which are described in the remainder of this book. A literal interpretation of Bible prophecy reveals how current world events are lining up precisely as the prophets described. Such world events include the formation of the European Union (EU) and its ten member Western European Union (WEU), the rise of China as a world power, the technology for implementing the "Mark of the Beast", widespread nuclear capability by rouge nations and terrorists, Jerusalem as the focus of the world's attention, the dramatic increase in earthquakes, restoration of the Hebrew language and the "unsealing" of the book of Daniel and Revelation. These are just a sample of events telling us that we are indeed in the last generation discussed so many times throughout the Bible.

THREE

WHY READ PROPHECY?

Luke 24:44: He said to them, "This is what I told you while I was still with you: Everything must be fulfilled that is written about me in the Law of Moses, the Prophets and the Psalms."

The words of Old Testament prophecy were of tremendous importance to Jesus. He not only quoted Old Testament prophecy at virtually every opportunity, but he also made a point to reference the fulfillment of prophecy as they actually occurred. These truths are evident even with a quick review of the four Gospels. The fact that Jesus spent such a considerable amount of time using prophecy in His everyday life is compelling, but more importantly, Jesus spent His last hours on earth, both before and after his resurrection, teaching prophecy. The Olivet Discourse (Matt 24/25, Mark 13, Luke 21), where Jesus expounded on prophecy pertaining to "the end of the age", occurred only two days before his arrest. From reading Luke 24, which contains a detailed description of events following the resurrection, it becomes clear that the focus of Christ's last words were of prophecy (Luke 24:25-27, 44-49).

These last teachings included the fact that Jesus considered it *"foolish"* not to have believed *"all that the prophets have spoken"* and He continued this teaching by explaining to his disciples that all of the prophecies about Him must be fulfilled. The very fact that Jesus choose to spend so much of His last remaining days on earth discussing prophecy should give ample proof that prophecy should not be ignored. There are many additional reasons that knowledge of prophecy should be a vital part of our Bible studies.

Significant Amount of Bible Devoted to Prophecy

According to many scholars, approximately 27-28% of the entire Bible is devoted to prophecy which is a staggering amount of text given to one particular subject (1, 2). Analysis of each prophecy, as shown by John Walvoord reveals that approximately 500 prophecies contained within the Bible have already been fulfilled in a literal way (3, 4). This fact alone should dispel the notion that prophecy should be understood in a non-literal way.

It has also been documented that within the New Testament, there are 318 references to the Lord's Second Coming, or stated another way, one of every 30 verses mentions Christ's return (5, 6). All but four of the New Testament books contain teachings on the Second Coming of Jesus. Again, the importance of these scriptures cannot be underestimated.

Considering the amount of text devoted to prophecy, and particularly the amount given to the Second Coming of Jesus Christ, it would be reasonable to assume that prophecy is important to God and therefore important for us to read and understand.

Fulfillment of Prophecy Devoted to Jesus First Coming

According to Grant Jeffrey, there are 48 specific and detailed prophecies involving the first coming of Jesus Christ (7, 8). Each of these prophecies was fulfilled in a literal manner. These prophecies reveal detailed and specific information about the birth and life of Jesus, followed by His death and resurrection. None of these prophecies were fulfilled in an allegorical or spiritual manner. A small sample representing the literal nature of these prophecies is given below:

- Micah 5:2: the Messiah to be born in Bethlehem (fulfillment: Matthew 2:1 which described Bethlehem as the birthplace of Christ).
- Isaiah 40:3: the birth of Jesus would be preceded by a messenger (fulfillment: Matthew 3:1-3, which detailed John the Baptist as this messenger).
- Zechariah 9:9: Jesus would enter Jerusalem on donkey/colt (fulfillment: Luke 19:35-37).
- Psalms 41:9: Jesus would be betrayed by "a familiar friend" (fulfillment: Matthew 26:47-48, when Judas betrayed Christ).
- Zechariah 11:12-13: A potter's field would be bought for 30 pieces of silver, the betrayal money, which Judas had thrown in the temple (fulfillment: Matthew 26:15 and 27:5-7).
- Isaiah 50:6 and 53:5: Both describe that Jesus would be scourged and spit upon before His death (fulfillment: Matthew

27:26; Mark 14:65 and Luke 22:63).
- Isaiah 53:7: Jesus would be silent before His accusers (fulfillment: Matthew 27:12-14).
- Psalms 34:20: Jesus' bones would not be broken at the crucifixion (fulfillment: John 19:33).
- Psalms 69:21, Jesus would be given vinegar to drink on the cross (fulfillment: Matthew 27:48).
- Psalms 22:16, which describe Jesus hands and feet pierced at the cross (fulfillment: Mark 15:24-25; Luke 23:33; John 19:23).
- Psalms 22:18: the soldiers at the cross would gamble for Jesus' garments (fulfillment: John 19: 23-2).
- Amos 8:9: Darkness would cover the earth during the crucifixion (fulfillment: Matthew 27: 45).

By reviewing these and other prophecies around the first coming of Christ, it is easy to understand the literal nature of prophecy. The literal fulfillment of these past prophecies give a strong and compelling reason to understand the words exactly as they are written, without adding additional "symbolic" meaning(s). One can read the words of prophecy with the assurance that these writings, recorded thousands of years ago by the Prophets, specifically chosen by God, will occur as written. The prophecies have been fulfilled in a very literal way in the past, thus there is no reason to believe that future prophecies should be interpreted in any other way.

Jesus and Prophecy

Jesus frequently referenced Old Testament prophecy in the Gospels. It was quite common for Jesus to mention the fulfillment of prophecies as they occurred. Jesus also frequently answered questions by referencing Old Testament prophecy. Review of Jesus' use of prophecy reveals three points: 1) Jesus extensive knowledge and common use of the words of prophecy, 2) the importance that Jesus placed on prophecy, and 3) the importance of literal interpretation of prophecy: in each instance of Jesus referencing prophecy, He interpreted the prophecy in a literal manner. As Jesus mentioned fulfillment of prophecies, as they occurred, He did so with a literal interpretation. Even a casual glance at the prophecies will indicate to the reader the vast number of occasions that Jesus referenced the Old Testament prophecies in His everyday life:

- **Luke 4:18-19**: This scripture reveals that Jesus had just returned to Nazareth, following the temptations in the wilderness. Jesus reads the following scripture in the synagogue (Isaiah 61:1-2). *"The spirit of the Lord is on me, because he has appointed me to preach the good news to the poor; He has sent me to proclaim freedom for the prisoners and recovery of sight for the blind, to release the oppressed, to proclaim the year of the Lord's favor."*

  Luke 4:21: *"This day is this scripture fulfilled in your hearing."*

This scripture contains significant information. According to the Gospel of Luke, the very first public reading from Jesus was from the book of Isaiah. This particular scripture referenced the fact that Jesus had come as the Messiah; however **Jesus did not complete the scripture**.

Missing is the second half (bolded) of Isaiah 61:2 *"To proclaim the year of the Lord's favor, **and the day of vengeance of our God"***. Why didn't Jesus finish reading this scripture? Jesus had come only to fulfill the first part of Isaiah's prophecy, *"the acceptable year of the Lord"* (a reference to Jesus first coming, and the subsequent "Church Age" or "Age of Grace"), but not to initiate *"...**the day of vengeance of our God"***, which is a reference to the Tribulation. This scripture also reveals that different "times" or prophecies can be revealed within one scripture; for instance in this scripture, the First Coming and Second Coming of Jesus are both referenced within the same verse. By reading only the first part of this prophecy, Jesus was indicating that his presence on earth was a fulfillment of Isaiah's writing – at least the first part of his prophecy. However, Jesus was also indicating that the last part of this prophecy *"...**and the day of vengeance of our God."*** was not part of the First Coming of Jesus – thus representing a future event.

- **Luke 7:20-22** and **Matthew 11:4**: John, while imprisoned by Herod, sends messengers to Jesus to confirm that Jesus indeed was the Messiah. Rather than answering by a simple "yes" or "no", Jesus preferred to answer these messengers by quoting Isaiah 35:5-6 and Isaiah 61:1 ***"Go back and report to John what you have seen and heard: The lame walk, those who have leprosy are cured, the deaf hear, the dead are raised, and the good news is preached to the poor."***

- **Luke 7:27**: *"This is the one about whom it is written: 'I will send my messenger ahead of you, who will prepare your way before you.'"* Here, Jesus references Malachi 3:1, which revealed the emergence of John the Baptist and his subsequent role.

- **Mark 11:17**: Jesus reacted to the money changers in the temple, and stated *"Is it not written: My house will be called a house of prayer for all nations? But you have made it 'a den of robbers.'"* In this scripture, Jesus references Isaiah 56:7.

- **Matthew 8:14-17**: With this scripture we see that Jesus had previously healed many people who had been brought to Him, and had just healed Peter's mother-in-law; *"This was to fulfill what was spoken through the prophet Isaiah: 'He took up our infirmities and carried our diseases.'"* Jesus referenced Isaiah 53:4 in this scripture, revealing that His performing miracles are fulfillment of Isaiah's prophecy.

- **Matthew 13:13-15**: Jesus explains His use of parables as fulfillment of prophecy, and quotes Isaiah 6:9 (also found in Deuteronomy 29:4; Jeremiah 5:21; Ezekiel 12:2). *"This is why I speak in parables...In them is fulfilled the prophecy of Isaiah: 'you will be ever hearing but never understanding; you will be ever seeing but never perceiving. For this people's heart has become calloused; they hardly hear with their ears, and they have closed their eyes. Otherwise they might see with their eyes, hear with their ears, understand with their hearts and turn, and I would heal them.'"*

- **Matthew 13:34-35**: This scripture references the frequency with which Jesus spoke to the crowd in parables. *"Jesus spoke all these things in parables; he did not say anything to them without using a parable. So it was fulfilled what was spoken through the prophet: 'I will open my mouth in parables, I will utter things hidden since the creation of the world.'"* In this verse, the narrative indicates that His use of parables fulfilled the prophecy given in Psalm 78.

- **Matthew 21:4-5**: As Jesus entered Jerusalem, He first sent two disciples to find a donkey for Him to ride upon entering Jerusalem. *"This took place to fulfill what was spoken through the prophet: Say to the daughter of Zion, 'See, your King comes to you, gentle and riding on a donkey, on a colt, the foal of a donkey.'"* This scripture indicated that Jesus riding into Jerusalem on a donkey (with a colt) gave fulfillment to the prophecy contained within Zechariah 9:9.

- **Mark 7:6**: The Pharisees were asking why Jesus and His disciples didn't follow the strict ceremonial washing of hands prior to eating. Jesus quoted Isaiah, *"Isaiah was right when he prophesied about you hypocrites; as it is written: 'These people honor me with their lips but their hearts are far from me. They worship me in vain; their teachings are but rules taught by men.' You have let go of the commands of God and are holding on to the traditions of men."* This scripture provides another situation where Jesus could have simply given a direct answer, but again, He chose to reference prophecy from Isaiah 29:13 in answering the Pharisees.

- **Matthew 24:15**: Jesus referenced Daniel (Daniel 9:27) in His Olivet Discourse (Jesus describing "End of the Age"). ***"So when you see standing in the holy place 'the abomination of desolation' spoken of by the prophet Daniel - let the reader understand..."*** In this very important prophetic scripture, Jesus clarifies and confirms Daniel's prophecy about the Antichrist and the events around his (the Antichrist) false proclamation that he is God.

One of the most important aspects about Jesus and His

use of prophecy are contained in **Luke 24**. In these passages, Jesus emphasizes the importance of understanding prophecy on two separate occasions. In Jesus' remaining time on earth, He spent considerable time focused on prophecy, specifically how the people of that time missed understanding the prophecies around His birth, life, death and resurrection. These scriptures, perhaps more than any others reveal the importance that Jesus placed on prophecy. We can also see Jesus indicating that **all** prophecies concerning Him will be fulfilled - including all future prophecies. This point gains additional importance with the realization that the vast majority of future prophecies are about Jesus and His return.

- **Luke 24:25-27**: As we read this passage we find the two men who were walking from Jerusalem to the village Emmaus, three days after the cross (just after the resurrection, of which they were unaware). Jesus asked them what they were discussing (Luke 24:17), and they indicated that they had "hoped" that Jesus would have redeemed Israel (Luke 24:21). Then Jesus said, *"How foolish you are, and how slow of heart to believe all that the prophets have spoken! Did not the Christ have to suffer these things and then enter his glory? And beginning with Moses and all the Prophets, he explained to them what was said in all the scriptures concerning himself."* According to Luke, these were among the first words spoken by Jesus after the resurrection. Jesus emphasized that very prophecy that has been written about Him will be fulfilled. Jesus used the words "all" three separate times above, *"all that the prophets have spoken"*, *"all the prophets"*, and, *"all the scriptures concerning himself."* This clearly reveals that not only **past** prophecies were fulfilled, but **future** prophecies about Jesus **will also be fulfilled.**

- **Luke 24:44-47**: Next, Jesus appears to His disciples and gives a similar message regarding prophecy; *"This is what I told you while I was still with you: 'Everything must be fulfilled that is written about me in the Law of Moses, the Prophets and the Psalms.' Then he opened their minds so they could understand the scriptures. He told them, 'This is what is written: The Christ will suffer and rise from the dead on the third day, and repentance and forgiveness of sins will be preached in his name to all nations, beginning at Jerusalem.'"* Again, the emphasis is placed on the fact that the disciples did not understand the Old Testament prophecies, thus Jesus had to *"open their minds"* so they could understand what they had missed. This scripture also underscores the fact that **everything** written in the prophecies must be fulfilled.

Lessons from Luke 24: 1) Jesus explains that they are foolish for not understanding the prophecies. 2) Jesus explains that they should understand ALL of what the prophets have spoken. 3) Jesus took significant time explaining the prophecies regarding His coming and most of His last words on earth were about prophecy. 4) Jesus explains that everything written by the prophets must be fulfilled.

Confirmation of God's Word

There is no other way to describe the amazing accuracy of vast amounts of prophecy, fulfilled over a period of thousands of years – other than a divine, omnipotent God who knows our future. Any time I look for reassurance in the true word of God, all I have to do is remember the vast array of prophecy that has been fulfilled literally and how the prophecies are again lining up exactly as the Bible foretold. This is a great source of comfort and hope. If the Bible is God's divine word to mankind, then it should offer some proof of this. One of the many proofs, perhaps the most important are contained within the words of prophecy, and their fulfillment. There is absolutely no way man alone could have made the various predictions contained within the Bible with 100% accuracy. Only God can know the future, and absolute proof is found in the words of His prophecy. The words of prophecy have given mankind an ongoing, living proof of the existence of God and proof of the Bible as a document that has been given to us directly from God.

Prophecy Reveals God's Overall Plan and the Future of the World

God has given us detailed information on the fate of the world and the events that would occur, leading up to the end of the age. Included in this plan is a clear vision that believers in Christ would be saved from the tribulation period, and that Jesus would come to take believers to the home which He has prepared for us. By reading God's prophetic word, we can understand the ultimate fate of the world and the fate of individual believers and non-believers. We can also see exactly how the world events will fall into place, and how we can know the "season" of these events. By understanding God's prophetic word, one can observe the overall plan that God has for man.

God also gives us important information on the judgments to come, in order to keep us away from such judgment. We can see this clearly in **2 Peter 3:8-9,** *"But do not forget this one thing, dear friends: With the Lord a day is like a thousand years, and a thousand years are like a day.*

The Lord is not slow in keeping his promise, as some under-stand slowness. He is patient with you, not wanting anyone to perish, but everyone to come to repentance."

We will also see that there will be a purpose for the Tribulation, and that millions will be saved during this period – the last period on the earth as we know it.

Prophecy Gives Us Important Warnings of False Prophets.

In virtually every main prophetic writing there are strong warnings against false teachings. This message, due to its redundancy seems to have great importance. Jesus, Paul, Peter and John all stressed that in the end times, or "latter days" the world would see the emergence of false teachings and false prophets which would lead many astray:

• Jesus, in the Olivet Discourse, gave us multiple warnings of false prophets and false teachings (Matthew 24, Luke 21).

Matthew 24:4: *"Watch out that no one deceives you. For many will come in my name, claiming, 'I am the Christ' and will deceive many."*

Matthew 24:10-11: *"At that time many will turn away from the faith and will betray and hate each other, and many false prophets will appear and deceive many."*

Matthew 24:23: *"At that time if anyone says to you 'Look, here is the Christ' or 'There he is' do not believe it. For false prophets will appear..."*

Luke 21:8: *"Watch out that you are not deceived."*

- Peter, who devoted his last writings to "end times", also gave us multiple warnings of false teachings (2 Peter 2:1-22).

  2 Peter 2:1-3: *"But there were also false prophets among the people, just as there will be false teachers among you. They will secretly introduce destructive heresies, even denying the sovereign Lord – and bring swift destruction on themselves. Many will follow their shameful ways and will bring the way of truth into dispute. In their greed then teachers will exploit you with stories they have made up."*

  2 Peter 2:12: *"But these men blaspheme in matters they do not understand. They are like brute beasts, creatures of instinct, born only to be caught and destroyed, and like beasts they too will perish."*

  2 Peter 2:18: *"For they mouth empty, boastful words and, by appealing to the lustful desires of sinful human nature, they entice people who are just escaping from those who live in error."*

- John, in his writings, gave us several warnings against false prophets and false teachings (1 John and 2 John).

  1 John 2:26: *"I am writing these things to you about those who are trying to lead you astray"*

  1 John 3:7: *"Dear children, do not let anyone lead you astray."*

1 John 4:1: *"Dear friends, do not believe every spirit, but test the spirits to see whether they are from God, because many false prophets have gone out into the world. This is how you can recognize the spirit of God: Every spirit that acknowledges that Jesus Christ has come in the flesh is from God, but every spirit that does not acknowledge Jesus is not from God. This is the spirit of the Antichrist..."*

- Paul also gave specific warnings against counterfeit miracles, signs and wonders (2 Thessalonians 2: 9-10).

2 Thessalonians 2:9-10: *"The coming of the lawless one will be in accordance with the work of Satan displayed in all kinds of counterfeit miracles, signs and wonders, and in every sort of evil that deceives those who are perishing. They perish because they refused to love the truth and so be saved."*

These warnings compel us to have a certain, fundamental, working knowledge of the Bible. Certainly, at a minimum, one should reference the Bible when faced with any sort of questionable teaching from the secular world and from their churches. Knowledge of the Bible is the only way to combat false teachings.

Prophecy Dictates Understanding of the Imminent Return of Christ.

By reading and understanding the prophecies written about the return of Christ, it is easy to see how we may very well be living in that very special time. The thought that Jesus will return, literally at any given moment is life changing. The concept that we should watch for His return and live as if it will be at any moment is given repetitively by Jesus in the scriptures. In addition, we are given abundant information regarding what events to watch for in the context of Christ's return.

- Jesus instructed us to watch for His return repetitively; In the Olivet Discourse alone, there are six specific references to "watch" or be on "guard" for His return (Luke 21:36, Mark 13:33, Mark 13:35, Mark 13:37, Matt. 24:42, Matt. 25:13)

Luke 21:36: *"Be always on the watch, and pray..."*

Mark 13:33: *"Be on guard! Be alert! You do not know when that time will come."*

Mark 13:35: *"Therefore keep watch..."*

Mark 13:37: *"What I say to you, I say to everyone: 'Watch!' "*

Matthew 24:42: *"Therefore keep watch because you do not know on what day your Lord will come."*

Matthew 25:13: *"Therefore keep watch, because you do not know the day or the hour."*

- There are four additional references about watching for the events, as described by Jesus, which will indicate that the Second Coming is approaching (Luke 21:28; Luke 21:31; Mark 13:29; Matthew 24:33).

Luke 21:28: *"When these things begin to take place, stand up and lift your heads, because your redemption is drawing near."*

Luke 21:31: *"Even so, when you see these things happening, you know that the Kingdom of God is near."*

Mark 13:29: *"Even so, when you see these things happening, you know that it is near, right at the door."*

Matthew 24:33: *"Even so, when you see all these things, you know that it is near, right at the door."*

"These things" refer to the various events that Jesus had just described which would inform us that His Second Coming is approaching. We will detail this information in the chapter entitled, "The Olivet Discourse".

• The imminent return of Christ should motivate believers to live enhanced lives and to witness on behalf of Christ (Revelation 1:3, 22:12).

Revelation 1:3: *"Blessed is the one who reads the words of this prophecy, and blessed are those who hear it and take to heart what is written in it, because the time is near."*

Revelation 22:12: *"Behold, I am coming soon! My reward is with me, and I will give everyone according to what he has done."*

Prophecy Gives Us Hope for the Future and Eliminates Fear

- There are four separate, distinct scriptures which indicate that Christians will be delivered or saved from the
wrath of God, or also known as the Tribulation ("wrath",
in the context of the scripture clearly refers to the
Tribulation). This seven year period, which is described
in detail in the book of Revelation (Chapters 6-18) will
be, according to Jesus, a time unequalled in any previous
history of the world:

  - 1 Thessalonians 1:9-10: *"....To serve the
living and true God , and to wait for his
Son from heaven, whom he raised from,
the dead - Jesus, who rescues us from
the coming wrath."*

  - 1 Thessalonians 5:9: *"For God did not
appoint us to suffer wrath..."*

  - Revelation 3:10: *"Since you have kept my
command to endure patiently, I will also
keep you from the hour of trial that is
going to come upon the whole world to
test those who live on earth."*

  - 2 Peter 2:9: *"If this is so, then the Lord
knows how to rescue godly men from
trials and to hold the unrighteous for the
Day of Judgment."*

Prophecy Should Not Be Neglected Because of the Importance Placed by God

The vast amount of the Bible which is devoted to prophecy should serve as a strong "hint" as to the importance placed by God on this topic. Why else would He devote so much text to this subject? Jesus informed us to watch for His return on multiple occasions. In His Olivet Discourse, Jesus gave us detailed information regarding the events that would be taking place just before His return. The only way to "watch" is to know and understand what exactly to watch for! This information is provided throughout the Bible – it is there for us to read and understand. To summarize:

- The significant percentage of the Bible devoted to prophecy (27-28%) reveals the importance of prophecy.

- A literal interpretation of future prophecy indicates that all "end time events", including the Rapture of the Church, the Tribulation and the Second Coming of Christ may be very near. Therefore prophecy should be important to us as part of "watching" as directed by Jesus.

- By understanding prophecy, we will know how to watch for the various events as they occur and we will know their significance in terms of God's plan.

We are Blessed/Rewarded for Watching and Longing for Christ's Return.

In addition to the multiple scriptures which tell us to watch and anticipate the return of Christ, we can find specific references to blessings which we will receive for this effort:

- **2 Timothy 4:8**: *"Now this is in store for me the **crown of Righteousness**, which the Lord, the righteous Judge, will reward to me on that day – and not only me, **but also all who have longed for his appearing.**"*

- **Revelation 1:3**: *"Blessed is the one who **reads the words** of this prophecy, and blessed are those who **hear it and take to heart** what is written in it, because the time is near."*

CHAPTER THREE NOTES

1. J. Barton Payne. Encyclopedia of Biblical Prophecy (New York; Harper and Row Publishers. 1973).

2. Tim LaHaye. The Merciful God of Prophecy: His Loving Plan for You in the End Times (LaHaye Publishing Group LLC. 2002).

3. John F. Walvoord. Prophecy in the New Millennium: A Fresh Look at Future Events (Kregel Publications. 2001).

4. John F. Walvoord. Every Prophecy of the Bible (Charist Victor Publishing. 1990, 1999).

5. Tim LaHaye and Thomas Ice. Charting the End Times. A Visual Guide to Understanding Bible Prophecy (Harvest House Publishers. 2001).

6. Tim LaHaye. Prophecy Study Bible (AMG Publishers. 2000).

7. Grant R. Jeffrey. Triumphant Return. The Coming Kingdom of God (Frontier Research Publications, Inc. 2001).

8. Grant R. Jeffrey. The Signature of God (Thomas Nelson Inc. – W Publishing Group. 1998).

FOUR

HOW TO INTERPRET PROPHECY

2 Peter 1:20: Above all, you must understand that no prophecy of Scripture came about by the prophet's own interpretation. For prophecy never had its origin in the will of man, but men spoke from God as they were carried along by the Holy Spirit.

The fundamental difference in prophecy interpretation is whether to understand prophecy in a literal manner or to create a meaning that isn't readily apparent from the actual words themselves. A summary of this issue is given below:

The Big Divide: Literal Understanding vs. Allegorical Interpretation

- **Literal:** To read any material in a literal manner, one assumes the author wrote the prophecy with the expectation that he would be understood as he wrote the words, with the "normal" meaning of the words. Literal interpretation also includes not adding additional, symbolic meanings to the text. This method acknowledges that prophetic language often contains figures of speech or symbols; however such symbols are explained or clarified in other parts of the Bible which are clearly "literal". This method allows the Bible to interpret itself and avoids subjective, human interpretation as much as possible (1). To summarize the method of literal interpretation we find the following ideas:

- Each word should be interpreted in the light of its normal, ordinary usage that was accepted in the times in which it was written.

- Each sentence should be interpreted according to the rules of grammar normally accepted when the document was written.

- Passages should be interpreted in the light of its historical and cultural environment.

- Analysis of the hundreds of fulfilled Old and New Testament prophecies reveal that all of these prophecies were fulfilled in a literal, specific manner. The 48 specific prophecies about Christ (specific prophecies about the birth, life, death and resurrection of Jesus) were all fulfilled literally (2). None were fulfilled in an allegorical or spiritual manner.

- The text itself should determine when literal interpretation is not possible, due to the nature of text (ex., dreams and visions, as written in the book of Daniel) look for the meaning to be given elsewhere. These types of scriptures are obvious and in each instance there is a clear meaning given later in scriptures or a clear reference to the meaning elsewhere in the Bible.

- Jesus interpreted Old Testament scripture literally in each of the many instances He referred to prophecy. In addition, Jesus' own prophecies, which He stated in the Gospels, have been fulfilled literally. The best example of this may be his prophecy regarding the future of Jerusalem in His description of "end times", Matthew 24:1, 2. Here, Jesus gave a seemingly allegorical statement *"And Jesus went out, and departed from the temple: and his disciples came to him to show him the buildings of the temple. And Jesus said unto them, 'Do you see all these things? I tell you the truth, not one stone here will be left on another; every one will be thrown down.' "* It would have been tempting at that time, to assume this was an allegory – particularly given the massive stones making up the temple, yet in 70 A.D. the Romans took down each stone to get the gold which had melted during the fires. It is also noteworthy that this is how Jesus chose to begin His "end times" discussion, with a specific prophecy which was fulfilled literally.

- **Allegorical:** This method of interpreting prophecy assumes that the scripture should be viewed as symbolic pictures of some spiritual truth – that the real meaning is different than the apparent meaning. This method was originally influenced by the desire to incorporate Greek philosophy into scriptures, and started during the third century and lasted throughout the Dark Ages, until the reformation – at which time the Bible was translated and made available for Christians to read for themselves (3). Allegorical interpretations include the view that the book of Revelation will not be literally fulfilled, but the book is simply a vague, symbolic view of good vs. evil. Allegorical views hold that none of the detailed descriptions of prophecies which are yet to be fulfilled, including prophecies about the coming Antichrist, False Prophet, Tribulation period, etc., will be fulfilled literally. To interpret future prophecy allegorically would require the belief that God would have one standard of interpretation for past prophecies (literal) and a different standard of interpretation (allegorical) for future prophecies.

Additional Clues for Reading/Interpreting Prophecy: 2 Peter

One of the great treasures in the Bible which relates to end time prophecy is found in 2 Peter. Interestingly, this was written not long before Peter was put to death, which further underscores its importance. Additionally, what is interesting about 2 Peter is the fact that Peter answers virtually every question or doubt that we hear regarding prophecy, particularly as the prophecy relates to our present age. It is amazing how many people in today's church refuse to take prophecy seriously, or refuse to even entertain the fact that we may be in the last generation of this age. The types of issues that Peter deals with in 2 Peter could have been written today. Below is a brief summary of his words which we should apply to our current age:

- **2 Peter 1:16-19:** These scriptures describe that fact that Peter had witnessed rather dramatic events during his time with Jesus, most notably the transfiguration (referencing Matthew 17). Here, as described in Matthew 17:1-13, Peter, James and John were led to a "high mountain" and witnessed Jesus, Moses and Elijah in their glorified bodies, *"There he was transfigured before them. His face shown like the sun, and his clothes became as white as the light. Just then, there appeared before them Moses and Elijah talking with Jesus."* However, in this passage found in 2 Peter, Peter states that the words of prophecy are even more certain than these events that he actually witnessed: *"And we have the word of the prophets made more certain, and you will do well to pay attention to it..."* Peter is telling us that the words of prophecy are even surer than the very events that we can see and hear.

- **2 Peter 1:20, 21:** *"Above all, you must understand that no prophecy of Scripture came about by the prophet's own interpretation. For prophecy never had its origin in the will of man, but men spoke from God, as they were carried along by the Holy Spirit."* This passage alone makes a compelling case for literal interpretation, because allegorical interpretations do require *"the will of man"* or *"the prophet's own interpretation"*. This scripture also confirms that prophecy not only comes from God, but that God expects us to understand that it is information coming directly from him.

- **2 Peter 2:** This chapter describes in great detail various warnings against false teachers and false prophets which was a common theme from Jesus, Paul and Peter in their end time writings. In addition, Peter gives us even more general information regarding end times prophecy in **2 Peter 2:5-8**: Here, Peter repeats the fact that the Flood was caused by God, yet he spared Noah and his family, *"if he did not spare the ancient world when he brought the flood on its ungodly people, **but protected Noah**, a preacher of righteousness, and seven others; if he condemned the cities of Sodom and Gomorrah by burning them to ashes, and made them an example of what is going to happen to the ungodly; **and if he rescued Lot, a righteous man,** who was distressed by the filthy lives of lawless men..."* Immediately following this description, we see in **2 Peter 2:9** that God will similarly spare his believers in Christ, or the Church from the Tribulation, *"**if this is so, then the Lord knows how to rescue Godly men from trials and to hold the unrighteous for the Day of Judgment."***

This is a very important point, because many Christians do not believe that we "deserve" to be spared from the "wrath" or the Tribulation. Their basis for this belief is the idea that Christians have faced persecution throughout the ages, so why should modern day Christians "deserve" to be spared? The answer to this question is provided by Peter. Peter tells us the following, 1) God has a history of protecting His followers from **His** wrath (upon those who do not repent) and, 2) God will protect His followers again, because He *"**knows how to rescue Godly men from...the day of judgment.**"* Another argument in terms of refuting the idea that modern day Christians don't "deserve" to be spared from the Tribulation is seen in the teachings of Christ. According to Jesus, any past persecution, etc. cannot be compared to the Tribulation, because the Tribulation will be like no other previous time on earth. Therefore, any attempts to make assumptions based on Christian persecution in the past have no relevance to the future judgments on earth.

- **2 Peter 3:2-6**: Peter now introduces the following topic - *"I want you to recall the words spoken in the past by the holy prophets...",* and then he proceeds to describe "scoffers": *"First of all, you must understand that in the last days scoffers will come, scoffing and following their own evil desires. They will say 'Where is the coming he promised? Ever since our fathers died, everything goes on as it has since the beginning of creation.' But they deliberately forget that long ago by God's word the heavens existed and the earth was formed out of water and by water. By these waters also the world of that time was deluged and destroyed."* Here, Peter tells us several things: a) Scoffers will say that previous generations did not see end times events unfold, as some had predicted, nor did the Second Coming of Christ occur, therefore it won't happen during the current generation. This is obviously flawed logic, yet we hear this daily – even from church leaders, and b) the same word that predicted the flood and fulfilled it, has also predicted future events which will occur just as stated scripturally. Also noteworthy, is that Peter picked a seemingly "difficult to believe literally" event, such as the flood to make his point – another reason to interpret prophecy literally. Further, Peter states that denial of literal interpretation, i.e., not believing in past events such as the flood, requires "deliberately forgetting". Ignoring the flood as divine intervention is not merely oversight, but actually requires consciously choosing not to believe. Ultimately, Peter is telling us to always remember that God is quite capable of causing "big" events to occur, such as the creation of the earth and the flood.

- **Revelation:** The book of revelation gives us additional information regarding reading and interpreting prophecy:

- In the description of seemingly allegorical scriptures, found in Revelation 19, 21, and 22 we are told how to interpret the actual words contained in these prophetic writings: **Revelation 19:9** states the following; *"Then the angel said to me 'Write: Blessed are those who are invited to the wedding supper of the Lamb!' and he added 'These are the true words of God.'"*

- **Revelation 21:5:** *"And he that sat upon the throne said, 'I am making everything new!' Then he said, 'Write this down, for these words are trustworthy and true.'"*

- These ideas are repeated yet again in **Revelation 22:6:** *"The angel said to me, 'These words are trustworthy and true. The Lord, the God of the spirits of the prophets, sent his angel to show his servants the things that must soon take place.'"* Note that the angel did not state that the words required man's interpretation, or that these words were merely spiritual meanings – rather he clearly stated that the actual words were trustworthy and true, just as written! God did not say "The symbolism of these words is trustworthy and true" but he stated *"These words are trustworthy and true"*! This requires a literal interpretation of the actual words themselves.

- **Revelation 22:18-19:** *"I warn everyone who hears the words of the prophecy of this book: **If anyone adds anything to them,** God will add to him the plagues described in this book. **And if anyone takes words away from this book of prophecy,** God will take away from him his share in the tree of life and in the holy city, which are described in this book."* Here, it is important to note that non-literal interpretation <u>does</u> require "adding" or "sub-tracting" to the scripture. This verse serves as a strong warning against this practice. By adding or inserting one's own interpretation, rather than simply understanding the specific words of scripture – one does change the original meaning by "interpretation".

As shown, it is relatively easy to prove that prophecy is of great importance throughout the Bible and we are now living in an age in which remaining prophecy is occurring exactly as a literal interpretation would tell us. The question that must be thoughtfully considered is this: Why would God give us this important information through His prophecy, yet make it difficult, if not impossible to decipher? Allegorical interpretation creates a scenario of widely differing and confusing "interpretation" with a high degree of ambiguity. Why would God leave these important words to man's own "interpretation"? With a literal understanding, the words do not change over time, and they do not change according to the reader. By understanding prophecy in a literal manner, we can simply read the words themselves and understand them, just as the example that Jesus set as He interpreted prophecy.

CHAPTER FOUR NOTES

1. Mark Hitchcock and Thomas Ice. The Truth Behind Left Behind (Multnomah Publishers, Inc. 2004).

2. Grant R. Jeffrey. Triumphant Return. The Coming Kingdom of God (Frontier Research Publications, Inc. 2001).

3. Dwight Pentecost. Things to Come. A Biblical Study in Eschatology (Dunham Publishing Co. 1958).

FIVE

WHY NOW? WHAT MAKES OUR GENERATION DIFFERENT?

Daniel 12:4: But you, Daniel, close up and seal the words of the scroll until the time of the end. Many will go here and there to increase knowledge.

Daniel 12:9-10: He replied, "Go your way Daniel, because the words are closed up and sealed until the time of the end...the wicked will continue to be wicked. None of the wicked will understand, but those who are wise will understand."

I must assume that it is easy for someone to say that we're not going to be "the generation" as described by Jesus in Matthew 24:34, simply because there haven't been "Old Testament" type miracles by the hand of God in over 2,000 years. The idea that we are not living in the last generation would seem the safe bet and certainly the least "controversial". I often wonder if many Christians, who refuse to even take a brief look at the current prophecies, simply decide to take this "safe bet" based upon these factors. Peter strongly rebuked these ideas as we just saw in 2 Peter 2:3-6, where he informed us that the flood actually **did** happen and Sodom and Gomorrah's destruction also **did** happen, and we will have a future *"day of judgment"*. He also warned that not remembering those times in which God demonstrated his power, such as the creation of the world, and later the flood, required actively and "deliberately" forgetting these truths.

There are at least ten specific "events" in the world now, all of which are necessary for end time prophecy to be fulfilled. All of these events or scenarios described have only occurred in our current generation, which allows observation by those alive on earth today. None of these essential prophetic occurrences were present during previous generations, and each of these scenarios should serve as a strong indication that we will experience the end time events as described by the prophets:

- **The formation of Israel in 1948**: Ezekiel 36, 37, and Isaiah 66:8 all describe the formation of the nation of Israel. This occurrence, the regathering of the people of Israel, was necessary for virtually all remaining prophecies to be fulfilled. In Ezekiel's day, there was no place called "Israel" because in Ezekiel's time - Israel had already been destroyed by the Assyrian empire at the beginning of the seventh century B.C. Yet, Ezekiel's prophecy contains multiple references to "Israel" and he also described Israel as a place that *"the people that are gathered out of the nations"* would come. This gives us a specific reference to the scattering of the Jews which began in 70 A.D., following the Roman siege of Jerusalem and lasted for approximately 2,000 years. This scenario was described by Ezekiel in Ezekiel 36:19: *"I dispersed them among the nations, and they were scattered through the countries; I judged them according to their conduct and their actions."* However, in the same chapter, Ezekiel describes a regathering of the people of Israel following this long exile in Ezekiel

36:24: ***"For I will take you out of the nations; I will gather you from all the countries and bring you back into your own land."*** In 1948 the world witnessed something unprecedented throughout history: a nation that had been destroyed and its people, who had been dispersed for centuries, was now miraculously regathered again. Literally overnight, on May 15, 1948, the nation of Israel was reborn. Ezekiel wrote extensively of Israel's regathering in the last days in chapters 36 and 37. Ezekiel 37 shows us a valley of dry bones. The dry bones represent the *"whole house of Israel"* that we are told will be restored in the last days. Ezekiel 37:21-22 tells us the following, ***"This is what the Sovereign Lord says: I will take the Israelites out of the nations where they have gone. I will gather them from all around and bring them back into their own land. I will make them one nation in the land, on the mountains of Israel."*** For approximately 2,000 years, the nation of Israel had been dispersed throughout the world. The fact that Ezekiel predicted Israel would again become a nation represents one of the most amazing, literal fulfillments of prophecy. **This singular event seems to have started God's prophetic end time clock, and is certainly one of the most important events which confirm that we are in the last generation.**

- **The formation of the EU and the ten-member WEU:** Daniel 2, 7; Revelation 17 all detail the same basic information. For the first time since the Roman Empire that existed during Jesus' day, we now have a literal revival of this Roman Empire in the form of the European Union (EU). In each of the pertinent scriptures from both Daniel and Revelation, we can clearly see how the Roman Empire must be revived in the last generation and specifically, that time immediately preceding the return of Jesus. Although this has been attempted many times in the past (Napoleon, Hitler, etc.), it has never successfully occurred. Now we finally have a literal revival of the old Roman Empire; the EU now has 25 member countries, representing over 450 million people. Geographically, it looks very similar to the ancient Roman Empire.

Additionally, we have seen the emergence of a powerful ten-member military "wing" within this revived Roman Empire, the "Western EU" or the WEU. The prophetic scriptures describe a scenario in which "ten kings" will rule with the Antichrist, and will exist for the primary purpose of supporting the Antichrist. We may be witnessing the rise of these "ten kings" as described in Daniel 7:24 and Revelation 17:12-14 in the form of the WEU. There is also one individual (Javier Solana) who holds the authority over this ten member WEU and has several other titles within the EU; 1) High Representative for the Common Security and Foreign Policy (CSFP), 2) Secretary General of the EU Council, 3) Secretary General of the WEU military alliance and recently has gained the EU version of "Homeland Security" with a "Defense Minister" serving under him. Javier Solana, with these titles has yet to receive a single vote from the european people – every position he now assumes has been so by appointment. He has by far the largest budget and the most authority of anyone else in the EU. He has the power to use military strength in the event of a "crisis" and these powers were granted in the EU recommendation 666 (1).

Javier Solana has also recently described his position as assuming the title of the EU President, once the EU constitution is ratified; in other words, the previous system of having a six-month rotating EU Presidency will end. He will assume that post as a permanent position once the constitution is ratified. This will amount in an unprecedented degree of world power with a single individual, particularly when considering that he has yet to receive even a single vote. While final ratification of the EU Constitution is being agreed upon, there are "emergency" powers which allow the WEU (under the direction of Javier Solana) to send troops where considered necessary. The rapid development and rise to power of the EU parallels the writings of Daniel 2, Daniel 7 and Revelation 17 in a precise manner. No previous generation witnessed such developments which are necessary for literal fulfillment of end time prophecies.

- **The technology to implement the "Mark of the Beast"**: Revelation 13:16. The company "Applied Digital Solutions" (ADS) has developed the capability to surgically implant a tiny computer chip, the size of a grain of rice into humans. This chip is capable of containing all financial information and all health related information for each individual receiving this implantation. Many people and vast numbers of animals have already been "chipped" with such a device. Through satellite technology, people receiving this chip can be tracked in terms of their specific location. There are "distribution centers" being planned within the U.S. for the purpose of implementing this technology. Additionally, a study was conducted by ADS, and it was determined that the optimal place on the body to insert this chip is in the hand or the forehead. We are the first generation to witness the ability to actually implement this "mark", which is described in Revelation 13:16, *"He also forced everyone, small and great, rich and poor, free and slave, to receive a mark on his right hand or on his forehead, so that no one could buy or sell unless he had the mark, which is the name of the beast or the number of his name."* We will see how the Antichrist will use this "mark" to seize control of the world economy and force allegiance to him (Revelation 13:16-17). Somehow this "mark" will also serve as an outward sign that the individual receiving it has determined his allegiance to the Antichrist, since it will bear *"the name of the beast or the number of his name."* Unfortunately, these people who do receive the "Mark of the Beast", will have sealed their ultimate fate as shown in **Revelation 14:9-10:** *"If any man worships the beast and his image and receives the mark in his forehead, or in his hand, the same shall drink of the wine of the wrath of God, which is poured out without mixture into the cup of His indignation; and he shall be tormented with fire and brimstone in the presence of the holy angels, and in the presence of the Lamb."*

- **Widespread (terrorist groups/nations) nuclear capability:** Zechariah 14:12, *"This is the plague with which the Lord will strike all the nations that fought against Jerusalem:* ***Their flesh will rot while they are still standing on their feet,*** *their eyes will rot in their sockets, and their tongues will rot in their mouths."* This scripture seems to describe the scenario of close range nuclear detonation. The neutron bomb, which represents a relatively recent development in nuclear technology, can explode with little resulting residual radiation. It is designed to kill humans, but to leave the surrounding area (including buildings etc.) untouched. Following the detonation of such a weapon, the immediate area can be inhabited almost immediately by humans. Importantly, and pertinent to this scripture, is the fact that the detonation of a neutron bomb – at close range – will consume human flesh in the same manner described in the scripture above. Additionally, a similar description of a more "traditional" nuclear detonation is given in Revelation 6: 14, ***"The sky receded like a scroll, rolling up, and every*** *mountain and island was removed from its place."* The next scripture, Revelation 6:15 describe a situation where *"kings of the earth, the princes, the generals, the rich, the mighty and every slave and every free man"* are hiding in caves and among the rocks of the mountains. This could be a description of attempts to escape nuclear radiation. This passage continues to describe darkness which is highly consistent with the nuclear winter that would take place following widespread nuclear detonations: *"The sun turned black like sackcloth...the whole moon turned blood red."* Interestingly, these descriptions occur just as John sees *"the stars in the sky fell to the earth"* which could be John seeing missiles as they reenter earth's atmosphere. Many of the additional judgments described in the book of Revelation also appear to result from nuclear detonations (Revelation 8:7 and 8:10-11) and further describe a "nuclear winter" which would follow multiple nuclear detonations (Revelation 8:12 and 16:8-9).

- **Jerusalem as the focus of the world's attention: Zechariah 12:3,** *"And in that day I will make Jerusalem a burdensome stone for all people: all that burden themselves with it shall be cut in pieces, though all the people of the earth be gathered against it."* Prior to the formation of Israel in 1948, the focus of the world's attention on Jerusalem was not possible. In 1967, Israel recaptured this land and at that point Jerusalem became the focus of the entire world. The violence and need for peace in the Middle-East has progressively dominated the news since that date. Now, because of the situation in the Middle-East, Jerusalem, and the conflict over this tiny piece of property is discussed almost daily in the news. This conflict also receives the considerable attention of world leaders, as resolution would end much of ongoing violence seen in the Middle-east. The fact that Zechariah prophesied this approximately 2,500 years ago is nothing short of amazing. It is also another sign that we are living in the last days on earth as we know it.

• Capability through **world-wide satellite television/ cable** to fulfill Revelation 11:1-12, to **observe the two witnesses sent by God during the Tribulation**: Revelation 11 gives us a great deal of information regarding the presence of two powerful individuals who will arise during the Tribulation. They will be given specific powers to bolster their ability to witness (and will prophesy for one-half of the Tribulation), such as the power to withhold rain and to turn the waters into blood. They will also be supernaturally protected during their period of witnessing. These two witnesses, who have been sent to Jerusalem by God, will proclaim the Gospel to the entire world. Following their designated period of witnessing (1,260 days), the Antichrist will have them killed. The entire world will witness this event, and then see their bodies for three and one-half days. The entire world will also witness their miraculous resurrection three days later. Until world-wide television, with cable and satellites this entire scenario was not possible. However, with the capability of satellite television now available throughout the world, and with 24 hour news shows running worldwide, it is easy to see how this prophecy will be fulfilled in a literal way. Revelation 11:9 reveals this truth, *"For three and a half days men from every people, tribe, language and nation will gaze on their bodies and refuse them burial."* In addition, we will see that the world will also witness their resurrection, Revelation 11:11, *"But after the three and a half days a breath of life from God entered them, and they stood on their feet, and terror* *struck those who saw them. Then they heard a loud voice from heaven saying to them, 'Come up here.' And they went up to heaven in a cloud, while their enemies looked on."* Until the world-wide availability of satellite television, this fulfillment would not have been possible, yet in today's world it is common for significant events to be witnesses in real-time by everyone with access to television.

- **The signs given by Jesus:** In the Olivet Discourse (Matthew 24/25, Mark 13 and Luke 21) Jesus described many significant events which would be occurring in the period during the last generation. Specifically, he mentioned **war and rumor of war, famines, pestilences, earthquakes, and persecution.** Jesus stated that the events would be like the process of the birth pains experienced during labor. As we know, the process of labor is a cyclic process; that is, the contractions and pain comes at intervals which increase in magnitude and frequency.

War and Rumors of War

Warfare has been present throughout the twentieth century like no other time in history. World War I caused over 8 million deaths. Because of modernized weapons and larger combat forces, World War II resulted in approximately 56 million deaths. Following these two world wars, the world witnessed a prolonged cold war between the two nuclear powers, the U.S. and the U.S.S.R. The threat of war was constant, with the very real possibility of global nuclear war – a scenario representing the ultimate "rumor" of war. The twentieth century brought more deaths from warfare than all other centuries combined.

Today, there are estimated to be over 37 active conflicts in the world, but more ominously are the threats of war: China threatening Taiwan, North Korea threatening South Korea and the mainland of the U.S. with missiles, possibly containing nuclear warheads, Israel threatening to destroy Iran's nuclear facility and Iran threatening to retaliate, India and Pakistan threatening use of their nuclear arsenals, the ongoing Middle-East conflict growing to include Syria and other neighboring countries, and the ever present U.S. war on terror with the potential to expand beyond Iraq.

Certainly, considering the focus of the world's attention and the weapons of mass destruction developed, one could consider the twentieth century as the century of warfare and rumors of war. For the first time in history, mankind has the ability to completely destroy the world. The daily news programs are dominated by the news of war and the speculation of war breaking out in various regions throughout the world. Just as Jesus predicted, not only do we see nations against nations, but "kingdom against kingdom" which represents the ethnic groups at war with each other. Currently the world has witnessed some of the worse atrocities since the holocaust, as a result of the ethnic warfare in Bosnia, Serbia, Sudan, Indonesia, and Iraq, just to name a few.

Famine

Because of the various floods, droughts, warfare, economic collapse, and food distribution problems in much of the world, famine has been a growing concern, particularly in developing countries. According to the UN, the number of malnourished people in the world increased from 540 million in 1979/1980 to 580 million in 1989/1990. Perhaps the most important factor in the famine problem is the growing number of refugees worldwide who are fleeing persecution, armed conflict, murder, rape, torture and mutilation. It has been estimated that there are currently 35 million such refugees which is more than the entire population of Canada (2). From 1979-1994 there were an estimated 6 million refugees fleeing from Afghanistan alone. Similar situations have existed in countries such as Rwanda, Iraq, Somalia, Bosnia, Sudan, Ethiopia, and Croatia, just to name several recent situations involving massive numbers of refugees experiencing famine. Many of the 3.7 million annual deaths in children are associated with malnutrition and the resulting inability to fight such infections as diarrhea, malaria, measles, HIV/AIDS and respiratory infections. As the number of refugees continues to increase due to the various conflicts around the world, the world's famine will continue to increase – another sign pertinent to our time.

Pestilence

There is a growing medical problem with not only newly emerging infectious diseases but antibiotic resistance to the existing infectious diseases. Additionally, several diseases once thought to be under control are now reemerging, such as tuberculosis, cholera and diphtheria. Infectious disease deaths in the U.S. had declined over the course of the first eight decades of the twentieth century, as a result of public health interventions. However the end of the century was marked by significant increases in infectious disease related deaths, despite even greater efforts in public health measures – an ominous trend for the future (3). The World Health Organization reports that at least 30 new diseases have been recognized just the last 20 years alone. At least 20 well known diseases, including tuberculosis, malaria and cholera have reemerged and spread since 1973, often in more virulent and drug resistant forms (4). Once thought almost eliminated as a public health problem, infectious diseases remain the leading cause of death worldwide. Infectious diseases account for most deaths across the globe, representing 34 % of all deaths annually (17 million deaths) and a staggering 71% of all deaths in children less than 5 years of age are due to various infections. According to the U.S. Department of Health and Human Services report in July 2004, HIV/AIDS alone has killed over 20 million people since 1981. More alarming however is the fact that 4.8 million people were diagnosed with HIV infections in 2003, which represents 14,000 new cases **per day**.

Resistance to these various diseases has become recognized by the World Health Organization. In a January 2002 fact sheet No. 194, the following facts were presented: *"The bacterial infections which contribute most to human disease are also those in which emerging and microbial resistance is most evident...The development of resistance to drugs commonly used to treat malaria is of particular concern, as is the emerging resistance to anti-HIV drugs...The consequences are severe...Most alarming of all are diseases where resistance is developing for virtually all currently available drugs, thus raising the spectra of a post-antibiotic era...Current trends suggest that some diseases will have no effective therapies within the next ten years."*

The magnitude of the growing threat from infectious diseases can be seen simply by looking at the numbers worldwide. Malaria infects over 500 million people across the globe. There are over four billion cases of acute diarrheal diseases annually, most in impoverished, developing countries where the impact is severe. It has been estimated that one-third of the entire world population is infected with tuberculosis, which causes over 2 million deaths annually. Clearly, pestilence is a sign of our times, just as Jesus predicted.

Persecution

Christian persecution is one of the most significant untold stories of the last decades of the twentieth century and into the present. There are several Christian groups who actively monitor Christian persecution throughout the world, including *Christian Persecution Information, International Christian Concern, Voice of the Martyrs, Christian Persecution Watch, and Christian Solidarity International* just to name five such organizations. It has been consistently estimated that over 150,000 Christians are killed annually because of their faith – an astonishing number. In addition to the Christian deaths, other forms of persecution are reported such as beatings, torture, imprisonment, sexual assault, and destruction of churches. In Sudan, there has been a "Christian genocide" taking place as entire villages are burned by Muslim extremists. Christians are asked to renounce their faith or face immediate death. Reports of these atrocities have included an array of countries including India, Nigeria, Sri Lanka, Turkey, Saudi Arabia, Pakistan, Iraq, Vietnam, Sudan, Nairobi, Egypt, and Indonesia. According to the *Christian News Service Daily Christian Magazine*, more Christians died for their faith in the twentieth century than all previous centuries combined.

Earthquakes

Jesus described these signs as occurring similarly to the process of labor or birth pains. This has been the case with earthquakes as recorded over the last century. According to the U.S. Geological Survey (USGS) earthquake database, earthquakes measuring greater than a 7.0 on the Richter Scale have had four peaks recorded over the past 100 years. One such peak occurred in the years clustered around 1910

(~1905-1915) and the next peak was recorded in the 1940's. Interestingly, these two peaks generally coincided with the two World Wars.

The next peak was seen in the early 1970's. Each of these three peaks in activity from 1910 to 1970 occurred at approximately 30 year intervals. The next observed peak was approximately 20 years later as the 1990's represented the next peak in earthquake activity. Considering this peak seen in the 1990's, it is interesting to observe that the long term average was also exceeded in the years 1992, 1995, 1996 and 1999. There had been no such increase since 1971 prior to the increase observed during the 1990's.

Jesus said that the earthquakes would occur in diverse places. According to the USGS – Earthquake Hazards Program, because of the huge increase in seismograph stations located worldwide (1931 = 350 stations; 2004 = over 8,000 stations) we can now locate thousands of earthquakes that would have previously been undetected. There are now approximately 20,000 earthquakes monitored annually throughout the world. These quakes will continue to increase in frequency and severity according to prophecy and will cumulate in one final, dramatic earthquake as described in Revelation 16:18: *"Then there came flashes of lightening, rumblings, peals of thunder and a severe earthquake. No earthquake like it has ever occurred since man has been on earth, so tremendous was the quake."*

Just as Jesus described, earthquakes are now being recognized in more "diverse places" than ever before and just at the same time the earth is experiencing an increase in overall activity.

• We know from both Daniel and Revelation that there will be a **200 million man army** originating from east of the river Euphrates, and this army will **cross the Euphrates**: Revelation 9:14-16 give the following description; *"It said to the sixth angel, who had the trumpet, 'Release the four angels who are bound at the great river Euphrates.'...The number of the mounted troops was two hundred million."* Revelation 16:12: *"The sixth angel poured out his bowl on the great river Euphrates, and its water was dried up to prepare the way for the kings from the East."*

Historically, the Euphrates River has been a significant military barrier dividing the East from the West. Now, for the first time in history, this huge river can be dammed. Turkey has recently completed the Ataturk Dam, which can completely dry up the Euphrates River. Additionally, the Chinese government has spent considerable efforts to build a super-highway across Asia, headed towards Israel. This highway stretches across the southern part of China, Tibet, Afghanistan and Pakistan (5). Towards the end of the Tribulation these troops will begin their move towards Israel. Daniel 11:44 describes the alarm experienced by the Antichrist with this army preparing to march across the Euphrates, *"But reports from the east...will alarm him, and he will set out in great rage to destroy and annihilate many."* Only recently has this number been reached by the armies and militias of the east. China alone has most likely achieved this number of 200 million troops (6) – certainly any additional armies from the East (North Korea?) would easily surpass this 200 million number. The biblical description of this 200 million man army represents a literal number which could not have occurred in any previous generation. The complete drying of the Euphrates River is now possible; another fact that differentiates the current generation from past generations.

- **Restoration of the Hebrew language** (Zephaniah 3:9). The prophet Zephaniah also made an amazing prediction.

Through this prophet, God stated that He would restore the ancient dead language of Hebrew as the spoken language of Israel. Hebrew had ceased to exist as the language of the Jews, even before the life of Christ. Hebrew is now the official language of Israel. This prophecy would not have been possible before the regathering of the nation of Israel in 1948.

* **The book of Daniel has been "unsealed"** for the first time and **the book of Revelation is understood (literally)** for the first time. Because of the recent explosion of books and commentaries which implement a literal interpretation of Daniel (and other prophetic writings) – the book has effectively become "unsealed": *"But you, Daniel, close up and seal the words of the scroll until the time of the end."* (Daniel 12:4) and *"Go your own way, Daniel, because the words are closed up and sealed until the time of the end."* (Daniel 12:10). Both the book of Daniel and the book of Revelation tell us that the books would remain sealed until "the time of the end".

The very fact that Daniel has become "unsealed" during our current generation is ample evidence that we are living in this special time. This is also proven by the vast array of prophecy books, movies, and literature and internet sites all dissecting and discussing the book of Daniel, along with the book of Revelation. This phenomenon is a very recent occurrence; certainly no previous generation has witnessed availability and popularity of these books on a literal basis. Hal Lindsey's "The Late Great Planet Earth", published in 1971, and was the first widely available book which took a literal interpretation of prophecy scriptures. Prior to this date, there had been writings confined to academic circles, but "The Late Great Planet Earth" was read by and discussed in the mainstream media. Since that time, there have been hundreds of books "opening" this information to the public.

Over the past several decades we have seen an unprecedented growth of information detailing the literal interpretation of these prophecies. There is similar wording in Revelation, where although this book was never to be "sealed", we can read where it would not be *understood* until the end time. Revelation 1:3, 22:7 and 22:20 confirm this idea. Revelation 1:3: *"Blessed is the one who reads the words of this prophecy and blessed are those who **hear it and take to heart what is written in it, because the time is near."***, Revelation 22:7, ***"Behold, I am coming soon! Blessed is he who keeps the words of the prophecy in this book."***, and Revelation 22:20, ***"he who testifies to these things says, 'Yes, I am coming soon.'"*** From these scriptures we can easily see that once people *"take to heart what is written"*, or in other terms, when people gain an understanding of these scriptures, then the time is near. In order to *testify* to something, one must first understand what is being testified. This scripture tells us that once the book of Revelation can be testified to, or understood, then, at that point, Jesus will be coming soon.

The past several decades represent the first such period in which there has been an explosion of information – on a wide scale, worldwide, revealing literal truths about both books. The "Left Behind" series by Tim LaHaye and Jerry Jenkins, which has been a best-seller for most of the last decade, has presented a literal interpretation of Revelation to millions world-wide. Never before in history has a mass dissemination and understanding of this book been not only made available, but widely read. This is but one example of the multitude of similar and related books. This phenomenon has never occurred before in history, particularly on such a massive scale.

These ten examples describe why our current generation is different from any previous generation in terms of understanding Bible prophecy. This particular list was used because it contains easily understood scripture, and events easily observed and documented. There are more extensive lists, but the ten above seem ample enough to make the point. It seems clear that there are many different factors making it obvious that we are indeed living in the generation that Jesus referred to in the Olivet Discourse. The fact that small minorities of well-intended (and some not so well intended) people have simply been wrong in the past does not provide a sound argument that we cannot correctly understand the season leading to the Second Coming, as described by Jesus. We must obey the commands given by Jesus to watch for his return. All of the events described should serve as a very strong warning that our "watching" may be fulfilled – and soon.

CHAPTER FIVE NOTES

1. Herbert L. Peters. Recommendation 666. The Rise of the Beast from the Sea. (iUniverse Inc. 2003).

2. Hillary Mayell. World Refugees Number 35 Million. National Geographic News. June 16, 2003.

3. M Wolf, KB Nolte, SS Yoon. Fatal Infectious Disease Surveillance in a Medical Examiner Database. Emerging Infectious Diseases. January 2004.

4. D Noah, G Fidas. The Global Infectious Disease Threat and Its Implications for the United States. National Intelligence Council NIE-17D, January 2000.

5. Grant Jeffery. The Signature of God (Thomas Nelson Inc., W Publishing Group. 1998).

6. Hal Lindsey. There's a New World Coming (Harvest House. 1984).

SIX

THE OLIVET DISCOURSE

Luke 21:28: When these things begin to take place, stand up and lift your heads, because your redemption is drawing near.

The Olivet Discourse (Matthew 24-25, Mark 13, and Luke 21) was Jesus' last major discourse and His most prophetic sermon. This teaching by Jesus outlines the general events which will be occurring in the "end times" and gives specific information about the Tribulation and the Second Coming. One way to view the overall outline of this discourse is as follows:

1) Signs of the latter days, in a general sense, including the beginning part of the Tribulation (Matthew 24:4-14).
2) The second half of the Tribulation (Matthew 24:15-28).
3) The Second Coming of Jesus (Matthew 24:29-31).
4) Jesus confirming that once the various "signs" are seen, then that generation will witness the concluding world events (Matthew 24:32-35). The "fig tree" from this passage may refer to the nation of Israel, thus representing the regathering of Israel. In this case, Jesus is saying that the generation which witnessed the 1948 formation of Israel as a nation, will be alive to witness the end time events.

5) The Rapture and a description of life at that time (Matthew 24:36-42).

6) Parables stressing watchfulness, preparedness, and faithfulness in the context of Christ returning (Matthew 24:43-51 and 25:1-46).

The Olivet Discourse, according to Matthew 26:1-2, was spoken two days prior to the Lord's death; it is striking that Jesus chooses to discuss prophecy in the few remaining moments that He had left on earth. Similarly, Jesus chose to discuss prophecy again, following the resurrection during the limited time He had left on earth (Luke 24). To summarize the Olivet Discourse we can see many important points:

• **Matthew 24:1, 2** - Jesus began with a seemingly "allegorical" prophecy which was fulfilled literally, *"Jesus left the temple and was walking away when his disciples came to him to call his attention to the buildings. 'Do you see all these things?' he asked. 'I tell you the truth, not one stone will be left on another; every one will be thrown down.'"* History records that these words were fulfilled literally in 70 A.D. when the Roman army destroyed the city of Jerusalem. Fires were burning throughout the city, including the temple area. After the flames diminished, it became apparent that large amounts of gold had melted and flowed into the crevices between the stone blocks in the temple. To recover the gold, the Roman soldiers took the stone blocks apart, stone by stone. Note that Jesus began His end time discussion with this prophecy – literally. How should the remainder of Jesus' prophecy be interpreted? It would seem that Jesus was giving us an indication with this scripture – a very literal interpretation of this prophecy was fulfilled. It would therefore seem quite reasonable that the remainder of the prophetic words of Jesus should be taken literally as well.

- **Matthew 24:3** - The disciples asked three questions: 1) *"when shall these things be?"* (the destruction of the temple), 2) *"what shall be the sign of your coming?"* and, 3) *"and (what shall be the sign) of the end of the age?"* Jesus answers each question specifically and literally in these relevant passages (Matthew 24-25, Mark 13 and Luke 21).

- Jesus warned repetitively about false teachers and their teachings, false prophets, deceivers and deception. In Matthew 24 alone there are six specific references to this topic (also see similar warnings given by Peter, in 2 Peter 2:1-22; by Paul in 2 Thessalonians 2:9-11; 2 Timothy 4:1-4 and by John in Revelation 2,13,17):

- **Matthew 24:4**: *"Watch out that no one deceives you."*

- **Matthew 24:5**: *"For many will come in my name, claiming, 'I am the Christ' and will deceive many."*

- **Matthew 24:11**: *"and many false prophets will appear and deceive many people."*

- **Matthew 24:23**: *"At that time if anyone says to you, 'Look, here is the Christ' or 'There he is' do not believe it."*

- **Matthew 24:24**: *"For false Christs and false prophets will appear and perform great signs and wonders, if possible, to deceive even the elect."*

- **Matthew 24:26**: *"Therefore if they say to you 'Look, He is in the desert!' do not go out; or 'Look, He is in the* *inner rooms' do not believe it."*

Just in the past 25 years we have seen the following major examples:

- Jim Jones followers in Guyana, 1978
- David Koresh and the Branch Davidians in Texas, 1993
- The Heaven's gate group in California, 1997
- The "new age" movement over the past 25 years
- "The Christ Mytraya" of England
- Cults
- Satanic movement
- Apostasy in the Church – false teachings that Christ is not the "only way" and that the God Allah (and of other religions) is the same God as the God of Christianity.
- "Jesus Seminar" group. False teachings of the gospels; redefine Jesus according to their beliefs.
- "The Last Temptation of Christ".
- The "Reverend Moon" and his movement.

- **Matthew 24:6-8**: *"You will hear of **wars** and **rumors of wars**, but see to it that you are not alarmed. Such things must happen, but the end is still to come. **Nation will rise against nation and kingdom against kingdom.** There will be **famines** and **earthquakes** in various places. All these things are the beginning of **birth pains**."*

Jesus described a scenario in which wars will be started by two single nations and then joined by "kingdoms" of the world, followed by pestilence/famine ("pestilence" was added to this list in Luke 21:11), and at the same general time, earthquakes will be experienced. More people have been killed due to warfare in the twentieth century than all other centuries. This was followed by the ultimate "rumor of war" as the 40 year cold war represented a prolonged threat of war which never occurred. Currently, as a daily part of the news, we hear of conflicts and potential conflicts occurring on a world-wide basis.

Large earthquakes as measured over a 7.0 on the Richter scale peaked in the early part of the century (~1910), then in the 1940's, again in the 1970's with perhaps the largest peak having just occurred in the 1990's. Now, unlike the previous 30 year interval between these peaks in activity, we are evolving into a briefer cycle of 20 years. These data are easily obtainable from the U.S. Geological Survey – Earthquake Hazards Program. Measuring these quakes annually, as compared with the long-term averages reveals that 1992, 1995, 1996, and 1999 each exceeded the annual average number for the century – an event that had not occurred since 1971. The deadliest earthquake of the twentieth century occurred in 1976, when "officially" over 250,000 people were killed in Tanhshan China. In addition, as a result of an increase in worldwide monitoring stations, we can see earthquakes occurring in diverse places like never before in history; just as Jesus predicted.

World-wide famine has reached unprecedented proportions (1), as a result of a combination of drought, floods, warfare and over-population. Tom Arnold, the CEO of *Concern Worldwide* stated in a press release on August 15, 2004 that because of hunger, 60% of all deaths in children less than 5 years of age are from diarrhea, malaria, measles and HIV/AIDS – a number equaling 3.7 million annually – all secondary to malnutrition. According to the *Center for Food and Nutrition Policy Worldwide Mortality Figures,* there were over 270,000 deaths from starvation in the year

2,000 alone. One of the greatest concerns for the next century is the massive number of refugees leaving countries engaged in ethnic cleansing and other forms of warfare. Currently there are millions of refugees from the conflicts in Bosnia, Sudan, Ethiopia, Croatia, Rwanda, Afghanistan and Iraq, just to mention a few.

There are now over 37.8 million people carrying a diagnosis of HIV/AIDS, with over 2.5 million deaths annually. According to the U.S. Department of Health and Human Services, by the year 2003 there had been an estimated 20 million deaths from HIV/AIDS alone (2). To contrast historically, the Bubonic Plague, also known as the "Black Death" killed approximately 25% of the entire population of Europe in the 14th century. This is considered as one of the worse plagues in human history; however the estimates of deaths from the Black Death were approximately 25 million – relatively speaking, a small number by today's standards. In 2003 alone, there were over 4.8 million new HIV infections diagnosed, which equals 14,000 new cases per day (2). Dr. Scott P. Lane of the U.C.L.A. School of Public Health and Department of Epidemiology reports that, in addition to the yearly AIDS deaths, there have also been approximately 4.4 million deaths from acute respiratory infections, 3.1 million deaths from diarrhea, including cholera, typhoid and dysentery, 3.1 million deaths from Tuberculosis, 1.5-2.7 million deaths from Malaria, 1.1 million deaths from hepatitis B, and 1 million deaths from measles (3, 4). Clearly, pestilences are on the rise world-wide and treatments may not be available in the near future.

The world population alone accounts for much of the dramatic increase in deaths from famine, infection and warfare. In A.D. 1, there were an estimated 300 million people living on earth. It took almost 1,600 years for this number to double to the 800 million people living in 1750. It only took about 150 years for the population to double again, as 1.7 billion people existed in the year 1900. Now the population doubles approximately every 40 years, as the increase from 1955 – 1996 was from 2.8 billion to 5.8 billion living people on earth. These numbers alone represent staggering possibilities in terms of the future of disease transmission, antibiotic resistance, famine and starvation.

The very fact that we have witnessed an escalation in all of these "signs" in recent history seems to confirm the idea that Jesus intended for this part of the Olivet Discourse to serve as general "signs" for the last generation, not as events strictly confined to the Tribulation. Each of the events that Jesus mentioned has indeed become newsworthy during the current generation.

• **Matthew 24:9-14**: *"Then you will be handed over to be **persecuted** and put to death, and **you will be hated** by all nations because of me. At that time many will turn away from the faith and will betray and hate each other and many **false prophets will appear** and deceive many people. Because of the increase in wickedness, the love of most will grow cold."* Considering end times events as analogous to "birth pains", it is easy to see how Christian persecution has grown world-wide during the twentieth century, as has the rise of false teachings. Although the persecution within the U.S. is often subtle, in the rest of the world there is intense persecution, particularly in Muslim states, Vietnam, Cambodia, China and Africa just to name a few. Several Christian news groups who monitor Christian persecution, consistently describe approximately 150,000 -160,000 deaths **annually** as a result of Christian persecution world-wide. As a contrast - during the Roman persecution of the first three centuries (after the time of Christ), lasting from 64 A.D. to 315 A.D. – estimates are given that 100,000 Christians were killed for their faith. **This**

number is now exceeded on an annual basis. Clearly, Christian persecution has reached epic proportions in our modern society. According to *Christian News Service – Daily Christian Magazine,* in Sudan alone, the Muslim government, in efforts to Islamize the population has taken the lives of approximately 2 million people who refused to convert to Islam. An additional 3.5 million are refugees. Jesus informed us that this process of persecution will intensify to even greater levels during the Tribulation.

- **Matthew 24:15-28**: This scripture gives a specific reference to the second half of the Tribulation, or known as "The Great Tribulation". The scripture tells us the following: *"So when you see standing in the holy place* **'the abomination of desolation'** *spoken of through the prophet Daniel – let the reader understand – Then let those who are in Judea flee to the mountains. Let no one on the roof of his house go down to take anything out of his house. Let no one in the field go back to get his cloak. How dreadful it will be in those days for pregnant women and nursing mothers! Pray that your flight will not take place in the winter or on the Sabbath.* **For then will there be great distress, unequalled from the beginning of the world until now** *– and never to be equaled again. If those days had not been cut short, no one would survive, but for the sake of the elect, those days will be shortened. At that time if anyone says to you, 'Look, here is the Christ!' Or, 'There he is' do not believe it. For false Christs and false prophets will appear and perform great signs and miracles, to deceive even the elect – if that were possible. See, I have told you so ahead of time.* **So if anyone tells you, 'There he is, out in the desert' do not go out; or 'Here he is, in the inner rooms' do not believe it. For as lightening that comes from the** *east is visible even in the west, so will be the coming of the Son of Man. Wherever there is a carcass, there the vultures will gather."*

In this passage, we have a specific reference to "the abomination of desolation" which is a description of the Antichrist claiming to be God, inside the rebuilt temple. This occurs at the mid-point in the Tribulation as the prophet Daniel had predicted: *"in the midst"* of the 70th week (Daniel 9:27). The length of the second half of Daniel's *"seventieth week"* is to be 42 months (Revelation 11:2, 12:6, 12:14, and Daniel 7:25). The distress refers to a combination of the intense persecution faced by those refusing to take the Mark of the Beast, and those refusing to worship the Antichrist, and it also refers to the last series of judgments.

These factors will make the last half of the Tribulation consist of "great distress, unequaled from the beginning of the world until now – and never to be equaled again." The passage continues to describe how people will be deceived during this part of the Tribulation, believing that the Antichrist is "the Christ". However, the scripture continues by clarifying certain clear distinctions which help identify the Antichrist as the Antichrist – not Christ. The last verses here clarify the issue: *"So if anyone tells you, 'There he is, out in the desert' do not go out; or 'Here he is, in the inner rooms' do not believe it. For as lightening that comes from the east is visible even in the west, so will be the coming of the Son of Man."* This message informs the Bible reader that Christ will only appear to earth in a visible, dramatic way. The Antichrist will not. This difference should allow the informed not to be deceived by the claims of the Antichrist. These differences are further described in the following scriptures.

- **Matthew 24:29-31**: In this passage, we find a detailed description of the specific events occurring at the time of the Second Coming of Jesus. These scriptures serve to contrast the manner in which Jesus will return and the uneventful rise of the Antichrist: *"Immediately after the distress of those days **the sun will be darkened,** and the **moon will not give its light; the stars will fall from the sky,** and the heavenly bodies will be shaken. At that time the sign of the **Son of Man will appear in the sky,** and all the nations of the earth will mourn. **They will see the Son of Man coming on the clouds of the sky, with power and great glory.** And he will send his angels with a loud trumpet call, and they will gather his elect from the four winds, from one end of the heavens to the other."*

Jesus repeats His warning that the **only** way He will return to earth is the same way He left the earth: Acts 1: 9-11, **"After he said this, he was taken up before their very eyes...They were looking intently up into the sky as he was going, when suddenly two men dressed in white stood beside them. 'Men of Galilee', they said, 'why do you stand here looking into the sky? This same Jesus, who has been taken from you into heaven, will come back in the same way you have seen him go into heaven.'"** This point seems to receive special emphasis, as the same message is repeated twice. We are to understand that Jesus will only return in the exact manner as described in the scriptures. Therefore, if someone claiming to be the Messiah, did **not** descend from the clouds and if that person was **not** seen doing this by the entire world, *"...as lightening that comes from the east is visible even in the west"* or similarly, *"...coming on the clouds of the sky, with power and great glory"*, **then it is not Jesus.** The Antichrist obviously will not come to earth in this way, thus, the wise will understand this important distinction, and will thus not be deceived. However, those people who are alive at the time of the revealing of the Antichrist, and unfamiliar with Bible prophecy will not understand this important distinction and will therefore be easily deceived.

- **Matthew 24:32-35**: Jesus now gives us the "lesson of the fig tree". *"Now learn this lesson from the fig tree: As soon as its twigs get tender and its leaves come out, you know that summer is near. Even so, when you see all these things, you know that it is near, right at the door. I tell you the truth; this generation will certainly not pass away until all these things have happened. Heaven and earth will pass away, but my words will never pass away."* There has been much discussion among evangelical leaders and scholars regarding the exact meaning of the fig tree. Currently, there are three main interpretations of this scripture:

  1) The fig tree represents Israel, thus, the same generation of people who witness Israel coming together as a nation (1948) – will also witness all of the events Jesus described, including the Tribulation and Second Coming (1). In today's world, a generation typically represents 70-75 years. There are several scriptural references to support this interpretation. In Jeremiah 24:5-6, just after Jeremiah describes the exile of Jews into Babylon, God showed Jeremiah two baskets of figs (representing "good" and "bad") and explained what the figs represented: *"This is what the Lord, The God of Israel, says 'Like these good figs, I regard as good the exiles from Judah, whom I sent away from this place to the land of the Babylonians. My eyes will watch over them for their*

good, and I will bring them back to this land.'" This is a reference to the Jewish people who had been exiled to Babylon. An additional reference is found in Hosea 9:10, *"When I found Israel, it was like finding grapes in the desert; when I saw your fathers, it was like seeing the early fruit on the fig tree."* Here, both the grapes and the early fruit of the fig tree convey God's delight in Israel when she, out of all the nations, committed to him in the covenant at Sinai. Matthew 21:18-21 also references the connection between Israel and the fig tree.

2) Jesus simply meant that generally speaking, just like leaves coming out or twigs getting tender in the spring, then you'll know that summer is near. Similarly, when you see the events that Jesus had just described in Matthew 24:1-31, you will know that the Second Coming is near.

3) Some scholars also believe that Jesus is only referencing the nation of Israel throughout the Olivet Discourse, thus, in this passage, Jesus is saying that when you see the events of the Tribulation occurring, then, that same generation will see the end of the age and the Second Coming of Christ.

All three of the above interpretations are basically giving the same information; that when we see all of the various events occurring, which Jesus had described (quite likely including the formation of Israel), then that generation would be alive to witness the end times events including the Rapture, the Tribulation and Second Coming of Jesus. By this general view, then the fulfillment of the signs (as given by Jesus in the preceding scriptures) would herald the coming of Jesus as certainly as the new shoots on the fig tree reveal the approach of summer.

The fact that Israel has been formed as a country during the time of these other "signs" seems to indicate that both ideas might apply; in other words, the fig tree could represent Israel being regathered (1948) and could also serve as a general representation of "the season" approaching as the leaves appear. Often, prophecy has duel meanings and this could be occurring with the parable of the fig tree. Interestingly, Israel has gained power and prominence over the last 50 years, which has been the same era as these other general "signs" as given by Jesus. This idea is bolstered by the fact that since 1948, all other prophecies have been lining up together as a unified orchestration. The rebirth of Israel in 1948 seems to have started the prophetic clock for the last generation, and certainly world events have confirmed that idea.

- **Matthew 24:36-42**: This is also one of the most interesting and debated passages within the Olivet Discourse. The question becomes a debate over whether these scriptures specifically reference the Rapture or reference the Second Coming: *"No one knows about that day or hour, not even the angels in heaven, nor the Son, but only the Father. **As it was in the days of Noah, so it will be at the coming of the Son of Man.** For in the days before the flood, people were eating and drinking, marrying and giving in marriage, up to the day Noah entered the ark; and they knew nothing about what would happen until the flood came and took them all away. That is how it* *will be at the coming of the Son of Man. Two men will be in the field; one will be taken and the other left. Two women will be grinding with a hand mill; one will be taken and the other left. Therefore keep watch because you do not know on what day your Lord will come."* This passage either references the Rapture, or the events around the Second Coming. The debate for each point of view is summarized below:

1) <u>Second Coming reference:</u> This point of view is tied into the concept that the entire Olivet Discourse should only be viewed in the context of Jesus addressing events specific to the nation of Israel during the Tribulation. Accordingly, Jesus' description of the general signs would relate solely to the first half of the Tribulation (Matthew 24:1-14) and the second half of the Tribulation is thus described in the remaining scriptures from Matthew 24 and 25. Thus, verses 36-42 could only pertain to the Tribulation at the time of the Second Coming. This view is seen as consistent with the parables given later in the discourse (Matthew 24:43-51 and Matthew 25:1-46) which would also only reference events of the Tribulation. Specifically then, the scriptures above (Matthew 24:36-42) would reference the aspect of the Second Coming in which believers will be separated from non-believers (Revelation 19:17-21). In this instance, the "taken" represent the non-believers who are removed from earth at the Second Coming and those "left"

represent the believers who will populate the earth for the next 1,000 years during the millennial reign of Christ. The reference to Noah would simply be a reference to the unpreparedness of those non-believers living during the Tribulation. This unexpectedness or lack of preparedness of the return of Christ is also referenced in verses 40-42 (5).

2) <u>Rapture reference:</u> This point of view maintains that Matthew 24:36-42 scriptures specifically reference the Rapture:

The following two verses (Matthew 24:36-37) seem highly inconsistent with events which will occur during the Second Coming: Matthew 24:36, *"No one knows about that day or hour..."* and 24:37, *"As it was in the day of Noah, so will it be at the coming of the Son of Man. For in the days before the flood, people were eating and drinking, marrying and giving in marriage, up to the day Noah entered the ark; and they knew nothing about what would happen until the flood came and took them all away".* Jesus had stated earlier in Matthew (Matthew 24:21) that the Tribulation would be like no other time in history, in terms of the mass carnage and "great distress", particularly at the end of the Tribulation, as there will be no water, little food, massive death and destruction. Therefore, it is hard to imagine that people will be merrily eating, drinking and giving in marriage (like the time of Noah). Matthew 24:37 gives a picture of life going on in a "normal" way which is hardly consistent with the end of the Tribulation. For these reasons, it is hard to imagine the scriptures are referencing the time at the end of the Tribulation.

If however, this entire scripture is referencing the time

just prior to the Rapture, then it seems to fit - we know the Rapture will come suddenly, without warning, and the Rapture will occur before the Tribulation. With a pre-Tribulation Rapture scenario, people will be going on normally in life, just as the time of Noah. For these reasons, Matthew 24:36-37 seem to be describing the time just preceding the Rapture, not the period of time at the end of the Tribulation.

Once the Tribulation begins, with the "confirming" of the covenant granting apparent peace in Israel, one can easily plot on a timeline the Second Coming of Christ because it will be seven years from this covenant signing. The Second Coming will also take place exactly three and one-half years after the "abomination of desolation", which will occur on a specific date – at the mid-point of the Tribulation. Therefore, it is hard to imagine the scripture as referencing the end of the Tribulation which will be an easily understood date. Matthew 24: 36 tells us *"No one knows about that day or hour."* For this reason, the idea that the entire Olivet Discourse is devoted only to the Tribulation seems impossible. However, if this scripture is a reference to the Rapture, then it seems to make more sense because the Rapture has no timelines and the Rapture will come unexpectedly just as described in the verse, *"No one knows about that day or hour."* This is a compelling reason to believe that Jesus was indeed discussing the Rapture within this passage of Matthew 24.

Additionally, the image of people literally disappearing from earth was given in Matthew 24:40-41, and contains a description which is virtually identical with other Rapture references given by Paul in 1 Thessalonians 4:16-17. Matthew 24:40-41: *"Two men will be in the field; one will be taken and the other left, two women will be grinding with a hand mill; one will be taken and the other left."* This seems to be a straightforward reference to the Rapture, without any inconsistencies.

However, to believe that this scripture describes the fate of non-believers at the Second Coming of Christ would contain inconsistencies. This image of non-believers as being "taken" at the Second Coming doesn't line up with the detailed Second Coming verses in Matthew 25:31-32, *"When the Son of Man comes in his glory, and all the angels with him, he will sit on his throne in heavenly glory. All the nations will be gathered before him, and he will separate the people one from another as a shepherd separates the sheep from the goats. He will put the sheep on his right and the goats on his left."* This verse doesn't allow for non-believers to have been "taken" at the Second Coming, because they must be present for this gathering before Christ. Therefore, verse 40-41 is far more consistent as a description of the Rapture rather than a description of events at the end of the Tribulation.

As an additional argument, in Revelation 19, the "lost" or the "non-believers", are not "taken" as suggested in #1 above, but are left for the birds to consume their flesh. Revelation 19:17 references this fate of non-believers at the Second Coming, *"And I saw an angel standing in the sun, who cried in a loud voice to all the birds flying in mid-air, 'Come, gather together for the great supper of God, so that you may eat the flesh of kings, generals, and mighty men, of horses and their riders, and the flesh of all people, free and slave, small and great.'"* This passage goes on to further confirm this idea in Revelation 19:21, *"The rest of them were killed with the sword.....and all the birds gorged themselves on their flesh."* From reading this literally, it does not appear that non-believers were "taken" simply because their bodies must still be present in order for the birds to eat their flesh.

Matthew 24:40-41 gives a description of a non-believer and a believer working together at the mill and working together in the field: *"Two men will be in the field; one will be taken and the other left, two women will be grinding with a hand mill; one will be taken and the other left."* Just before the Rapture and before the Tribulation, this is easy to imagine, as Christians and non-Christians obviously work together in such a manner. However unlike the time just before the Rapture, during the Tribulation intense persecution of Christians will take place. On this basis, it is hard to imagine that a believer and non-believer will be working together in a "normal" manner during the Tribulation – particularly just prior to the Second Coming. The intense persecution during the Tribulation is described in Mark 13:9, *"You must be on your guard. You will be handed over to the local councils and flogged in the synagogues"* and Mark 13:12, *"Brother will betray brother, and a father his child. Children will rebel against their parents and have them put to death. All men will hate you because of me..."* This severe persecution seems highly inconsistent with the idea that these two groups of people (believers and non-believers) will simply be going about their usual business like the days of Noah during the final stages of the Tribulation. However, **prior** to the Tribulation, the idea of believers and non-believers working together in this manner is far more plausible. This would also add to the array of scriptures which argue for a pre-Tribulation Rapture.

For all of these reasons given, I believe the preponderance of evidence points to Matthew 24:36-42 as being a reference to the Rapture. Matthew 24:36-39 describe life going on as usual just before the Rapture, with no specific signs or prophecy foretelling the Rapture. These verses describe life just on earth as being exactly like life at the time of Noah – business as usual. Matthew 24: 40-42 serves as a perfect description of the Rapture itself. Verse 42 closes this thought (describing the Rapture) by repeating the message that it will occur at an unknown time, *"Therefore keep watch, because you do not know on what day your*

Lord will come." This verse again contrasts with the Second Coming – a time which can be predicted based on the 7 year period beginning with the Antichrist confirming the "peace-plan" in the Middle-East.

- **Matthew 24:43-51 and Matthew 25:1-46**: There are five parables given by Jesus which conclude the Olivet Discourse. The main themes, which are repeated throughout these parables are instructions on being **watchful, faithful and prepared** during the last days which precede the return of Christ:

  1) **Matthew 24:43-44**: This parable consists of the watchful owner and his house. If the owner had received information that a thief was coming, he would have watched. Christ's emphasis here was about the fore-warning that the owner of the house should have recognized. The owner of the house was not "watching", thus he was broken into. Message: *"So you also must be ready, because the Son of Man will come at an hour when you do not expect him."* The application intended by Christ was this: those who see the signs would have a warning of the nearness of the Second Coming of Christ. Having been warned, they should be prepared for His coming, just as the owner of the house should have prepared for the thief. Thus, this parable stresses *watchfulness and preparedness*.

  2) **Matthew 24:45-51**: This parable stresses the need for **faithfulness** by those individuals who will witness the signs given

by Jesus. The parable is of the servant who was put in charge of the master's house. The Lord refers to a master – who before his departure gave specific instructions to the servant under his authority. This servant was expected to carry out his duties faithfully, and if found faithful, would be given additional responsibilities. By contrast, this parable gives a stern warning against not being faithful simply because the master has not returned, or has stayed away a long time.

The parable instructs those who witness the signs should be diligent and faithful **even though the Lord is absent**. This parable stresses that although the time of the master's return is unknown - that is no excuse for "wicked" behavior on the part of this servant. The overall message given here is seen in verse 50: *"The master of that servant will come on a day when he does not expect him and at an hour he is not aware of."*

3) **Matthew 25:1-13**: This parable describes the ten virgins who were awaiting the presence of the bridegroom and his bride at the place where the wedding banquet would be held. The ten virgins were divided into two classes: the foolish and the wise. The "foolish" virgins had made no provision for the bridegrooms delay, and the "wise" virgins, had taken extra oil in the event of a delay. Because of the delay, the virgins slept. Once the bridegroom appeared, the wise virgins had the necessary oil to go out and meet the bridegroom. The foolish were unable to

go out and meet the bridegroom because they had not prepared, and thus had no oil left. They now spent their time attempting to acquire oil, but it was too late.

This parable stresses that the virgins who were "ready" went in to the wedding banquet: *"The virgins who were ready went in with him to the wedding banquet. And the door was shut."* Message: *"Therefore keep watch, because you do not know the day or the hour."* Just as the scripture tells us, the "prepared" will be received into the kingdom and the "unprepared" will be excluded from the kingdom. Thus, this parable stresses the need to be **prepared** spiritually during the final days.

4) **Matthew 25:14-30**: This parable is known as the parable of the talents (a sum of money). Each of three servants was given talents according to his abilities. After giving out the talents the master went on a journey with the expectation that the servants would be faithful to the trust he had granted them. When the master returned, he saw that two of his servants had been faithful because they had doubled their talents. The master rewarded their efforts, **"Well done good and faithful servant! You have been faithful with a few things; I will put you in charge of many things."** However, in contrast to this, Christ proceeded to reveal the results of being unfaithful to the servant who did nothing with his talent, **"You wicked and lazy servant!"** Because he had done nothing with the gifts given to him, he was

considered as unfaithful, and was thus excluded from his master's household.

In this parable, Christ is teaching that those who see the forewarning of Christ's appearance and have an opportunity to prepare themselves spiritually need to do so, and will be rewarded when they do. For those who neglect the warnings in these signs (of Christ's return), and as a result, ignore the possibility of faith in Christ will be barred from the kingdom. Message: *"For everyone who has will be given more and he will have abundance. Whoever does not have, even what he has will be taken from him."* The parable then reveals that there will be rewards for those with **faithfulness** and judgment for those lacking faith.

5) **Matthew 25:31-46**: This parable is known as the parable of the separation of the sheep and the goats. Here, Christ is dealing with the issue of Gentiles during the judgment period of the Second Coming. Verse 31 seems to reinforce this idea: *"When the Son of Man comes in his glory..."* According to Dwight Pentecost (6), those who had faith will demonstrate it by taking the risk of helping persecuted believer: *"Whatever you did for one of the least of these brothers* (feeding the hungry, giving clothing to strangers, looking after the sick, etc.) *of mine, you did for me"* and *"...whatever you did not do for one of the least of these, you did not do for me."* Their **faithfulness**, as demonstrated by performing these acts of compassion, will grant them acceptance into His kingdom. Those

without faith, as demonstrated by ignoring the needs of persecuted believers will be excluded from His kingdom.

In summary, the themes of watchfulness, preparedness and faithfulness are the three main points demonstrated in these parables. These central themes are repeated on multiple occasions in these parables. There are multiple references towards "watching" or being "on guard" or being "ready" for the return of Christ:

1) **Matthew 24:42**: *"Therefore keep watch because you do not know on what day your Lord will come"*

2) **Matthew 24:44**: *"So you must also be ready, because the Son of Man will come at an hour when you do not expect him."*

3) **Matthew 25:13**: *"Therefore keep watch because you do not know the hour."*

4) **Mark 13:33**: *"Be on guard! Be alert! You do not know when that time will come."*

5) **Mark 13:35**: *"Therefore keep watch because you do not know when the owner of the house will come back..."*

6) **Mark 13:37**: *"What I say to you, I say to everyone: 'Watch!'"*

7) **Luke 21:36**: *"Be always on the watch and pray..."*

What exactly does Jesus mean when He tells us to watch? Clearly, in the context of the overall message within the Olivet Discourse, He is referring to watching for His return. So how does one obey this command by Jesus? Certainly he didn't mean to sit at a window gazing at the clouds for his return. Obviously it means to watch for all the various signs that he gave us in these scriptures. The way to do this is to watch and read the pertinent news reports of the various world events which may apply to the information Jesus gave to us. This also implies knowing how to apply the current events to the scriptures, which means we must know the actual scriptures! Jesus was very clear (and redundant) regarding this point! These points are consistent with the message in 2 Timothy 4:8:

> *"Now there is in store for me the crown of righteousness, which the Lord, the righteous Judge, will award to me on that day – and not only to me, but also all who have longed for his appearing."*

By "watching" we also reveal our deep love for Jesus, as we are anxious for His return in order to simply be with him and to be in His presence. As the current events lead us to believe His coming is near, we grow excited with the anticipation that we will soon be in His presence. This is no different than awaiting the presence of a loved one or family member who has been gone a long time. Who doesn't constantly look for that flight to arrive, by watching the airport monitors? Or waiting for the car to pull into the driveway by constantly checking from the window? Waiting and watching for Jesus to return is no different - only we watch current events in the world to line up as Jesus informed us. Jesus was very clear that He expects His Church to be watching and waiting for the Second Coming.

By doing this, we fulfill His requests (as shown in the parables discussed) to **watch**, to be **faithful** and to be **prepared.**

CHAPTER SIX NOTES

1. Grant R. Jeffrey. Triumphant Return. The Coming Kingdom of God (Frontier Research Publications, Inc. 2001).

2. United States Department of Health and Human Services. National Institutes of Health. July 4, 2004.

3. Scott P. Lane, MD. Principles of Infectious Diseases. UCLA School of Epidemiology/EPI 220. Department of Epidemiology. 2003.

4. CJL Murray, AD Lopez. Mortality by Cause for Eight Regions of the World: Global Burden of Disease Study. Lancet 1997; 349:1269-1276.

5. Dwight Pentecost. Things to Come. A Biblical Study in Eschatology (Dunham Publishing Co. 1958).

6. Dwight Pentecost. The Parables of Jesus (Zondervan Publishing House. 1982).

SEVEN

DANIEL

================

Daniel 12:9: He replied, "Go your own way, Daniel, because the words are closed up and sealed until the time of the end. Many will be purified, made spotless and refined, but the wicked will continue to be wicked. None of the wicked will understand, but those who are wise will understand."

The book of Daniel is one of the most significant prophetic books in the Old Testament, particularly as it pertains to current world events. Daniel had been taken into captivity as a 15 year old youth after King Nebuchadnezzar of Babylon conquered Jerusalem. This book contains a basic prophetic outline regarding key world events taking place from the time of Daniel (6th century BC) until the coming of the Messiah's kingdom. In Daniel 2 and 7 we get an overview of the four, world-ruling gentile kingdoms that would play an important role, not only in world history, but particularly in Israel's history. Interestingly, the most attention is given to the last gentile kingdom – the revival of the Roman Empire and the subsequent rise of the Antichrist.

Chapter 9 gives further detail, and also includes specific information regarding both the Antichrist and the "timelines" for significant, world-wide events. It is important to remember that the book of Revelation contains information which is not only consistent with Daniel, but contains greater detail for prophecy contained within Daniel, as well as explanations. For this reason, certain sections of Revelation must be read along with Daniel in order to see the complete picture. The same holds true when reading Revelation; during a study of Revelation, the pertinent scriptures contained within Daniel must be read for proper context. The focus of this chapter will be on the prophecies made by Daniel as they apply to today's time, but a brief synopsis of the other chapters will be given for the purposes of continuity.

Chapter 1: This chapter contains a basic description of Daniel being taken into captivity in Babylon, along with Shadrach, Meshach, and Abednego. These individuals are introduced in the following scriptures: Daniel 1:17, *"As for these four children, God gave them knowledge and understanding of all kinds of literature and learning. And Daniel could understand visions and dreams of all kinds."* Daniel 1:20, *"In every matter of wisdom and understanding about which the King questioned them, he found them ten times better than all the magicians and enchanters in his whole kingdom."*

Chapter 2: The chapter describes disturbing dreams that Nebuchadnezzar experienced. Because of these dreams his mind was "troubled" and he "could not sleep". He called his "magicians, astrologers and sorcerers" to interpret his dreams. Because they were unable to interpret his dreams, the King became angry and ordered the execution of all of the wise men of Babylon: Daniel 2:12 *"This made the king so angry and furious that he ordered the execution of all wise men of Babylon."* Following this order, Daniel spoke to the King's commander Arioch, and later went to King Nebuchadnezzar to request time to interpret his dreams: Daniel 2:16 *"At this, Daniel went to the king and asked for time, so that he might interpret the dream for him."* That evening Daniel received a vision: Daniel 2:19 *"During the night the mystery was revealed to Daniel in a vision."*

The next move was for Daniel to present his interpretation: Daniel 2:24, *"Then Daniel went to Arioch, whom the king had appointed to execute the wise men of Babylon, and said to him, 'Do not execute the wise men of Babylon. Take me to the king, and I will interpret the dream for him.'"*

The Dream: (Daniel 2:31-35 and Daniel 2:37-45)

In these scriptures, Daniel proceeds to describe the dream to King Nebuchadnezzar, which consisted of the vision of a large statue as described below:

- **Large statue**: described as "enormous", "dazzling", and "awesome".
- **Head**: Pure Gold = King Nebuchadnezzar and the Babylonian empire (612-539 B.C.)
- **Chest/arms**: Silver = "after you, another kingdom" = Medo-Persian empire (538-331 B.C.)
- **Belly/thighs**: Bronze = "Next, a third kingdom" = Greek Empire (330-63 B.C.)
- **Legs**: Iron = "Finally, there will be a fourth Kingdom" = Rome (I) - (63 B.C.-476 A.D.)
- **Feet**: partly Iron and partly Baked Clay = Rome (II), as Revived Roman Empire = Future Tribulation.

These four consecutive gentile kingdoms are represented by first the Babylonian Empire (gold), who was conquered by the combined Medo-Persian Empire (silver), who was subsequently conquered by the Greek Empire (bronze), which was led by Alexander the Great. At the death of Alexander the Great, this Greek kingdom was divided into four parts, which were all eventually taken over by the Roman Empire (iron). Interestingly, this last empire, the Roman Empire was described as being made of iron, but later would become a combination of iron and clay.

Daniel 2:41: *"Just as you saw that the feet and toes were partly of baked clay and partly of iron, so this kingdom will be a divided kingdom; yet it will have some of the strength of iron in it, even as you saw iron mixed with clay. As the toes were partly iron and partly clay, so this kingdom will be partly strong and partly brittle. **And just as you saw the iron mixed with baked clay, so the people will be a mixture and will not remain united,** any more than iron mixes with clay."*

The scriptures above, which give a description of the feet and toes of this statue, describe this Roman Empire as very different from the first Roman Empire, which was described as solid iron. This first part of the Roman Empire, described as legs made of solid iron is clear reference to the first Roman Empire that existed at the time of Christ. At that time, the Roman Empire would occupy its captive countries and rule with "iron". Their power and authority was absolute over the occupied land.

However, as contrasted with the description of "iron" representing the original Roman Empire, we see a different version of the Roman Empire which will rule at the time of the Second Coming. The scripture reveals that the feet and toes describing this empire would be made of a mixture of clay and iron. This description is clarified as a representation of the fact that *"the people will be a mixture and will not remain united, any more than iron mixes with clay."* The current European Union matches this description perfectly as the various countries within the EU are currently maintaining their basic sovereignty, yet they are allied with the other EU countries. Soon, they will have a unified, single constitution.

The modern EU geographically looks very similar to the original Roman Empire, but it is far more like "iron mixed with clay" politically. Because Daniel was describing successive empires, we know it began in 63 B.C., when the last of the Greek divisions was defeated. The meaning of the transition from iron to iron mixed with clay must therefore represent a different, future Roman Empire. In the eyes of some scholars, because the Roman Empire was never conquered (it took hundreds of years to gradually dissipate), it is considered that Daniel saw the "Roman Empire" over this vast period of time as it transitioned into modern day Europe (1). With this interpretation, this Roman Empire would gain strength again for the final seven years of Daniel's "timeline" given in Chapter 9. A second widely held opinion is that the Roman Empire would gradually end during the first century A.D., and then be reunified, forming a new "Revived" Roman Empire.

The scriptures indicate that this Roman Empire - whether it is a reunited empire or an empire that reemerges after this long period of impotence - will regain power just prior to the Second Coming. The evidence of this is given with Daniel 2:34.

- Following this description of the statue, Daniel 2:34 gives key information about the fate of this revived Roman Empire: *"While you were watching, a rock was cut out, but not by human hands. It struck the statue on its feet of iron and clay and smashed them. Then the iron, the clay, the bronze, the silver, and the gold were broken into pieces at the same time and became like chaff on the threshing floor in the summer. The wind swept them away without leaving a trace. But the rock that struck the statue became a huge mountain and filled the whole earth."*

• The interpretation of the scripture above is given in Daniel 2: 44-45 *"In the time of those kings, the God of heaven will set up a kingdom that will never be destroyed, nor will it be left to another people. It will crush all those kingdoms and bring them to an end, but it will itself endure forever. This is the meaning of the vision of the rock cut out of a mountain, but not by human hands – a rock that broke the iron, the bronze, the clay, the silver and the gold to pieces."* Daniel 2:45: *"The great God has shown the king what will take place in the future. The dream is true and the interpretation is trustworthy."*

These scriptures describe the "stone", which is of divine origin and the "mountain" which is a biblical symbol of a kingdom (see Isaiah 2:2, Jeremiah 51:25 and Ezekiel 20:40). The stone and the mountain represent the Kingdom of God that will replace all human empires, following the destruction of the final empire (the "revived" Roman Empire), as governed by the Antichrist. These events will then lead to the establishment of Christ's Millennial Reign.

To summarize this important chapter we can see that Daniel was given an interpretation of the King's dream. The interpretation described four successive World Empires, as they would rule over Israel, beginning with King Nebuchadnezzar and the Babylonian Empire and ending with the Roman Empire. The Roman Empire is described as being in existence in 63 B.C., because it succeeded the Greek Empire. The Roman Empire is also seen by Daniel as being in existence at the time of the Second Coming of Christ; therefore a revival of the original Roman Empire must take place sometime prior to the Second Coming. The current European Union fits the description of this revived

Roman Empire both politically and geographically. This last version of the Roman Empire will be destroyed by Christ at the Second Coming and this destruction will then usher in the 1,000 year reign of Christ on earth.

As a footnote, and for an interesting parallel to these last words, Daniel 2: 45 begins with the phrase *"The great God has shown the king what will take place in the future."* Following this introduction, the scripture continues with the following: *"The dream is true and the interpretation is trustworthy."* One can see similar scriptures in Revelation 19:9, Revelation 21:5 and Revelation 22:6 – however, note that in Revelation, the scripture states that the **"words"** are trustworthy and true, not the **"interpretation"**. This underscores the difference in a literal interpretation of a dream/vision (Daniel 2) and a literal interpretation of the "words" themselves (Revelation 21, 22).

Chapter 3: This chapter describes King Nebuchadnezzar setting up a large statue to be worshipped. Because Shadrach, Meshach and Abednego refused, they were sent to the fiery furnace. However, as seen in Daniel 3:26-27 *"Shadrach. Meshach and Abednego came out of the fire...the fire had not harmed their bodies, nor a hair of their heads singed; their robes were not scorched and there was no smell of fire on them."*

Chapter 4: This chapter details the important events in the life of King Nebuchadnezzar following another disturbing dream that he had experienced. Daniel again interprets the dream (Daniel 4:24-28), and this dream/interpretation was literally fulfilled in Daniel 4:28-37. The events which occurred are described as follows in Daniel 4:31-34: *"...a voice came from heaven. 'This is what is decreed for you, King Nebuchadnezzar: Your royal authority has been taken from you. You will be driven away from people and will live* *with the wild animals; you will eat grass like cattle. Seven times will pass by for you until you acknowledge that the Most High is sovereign over the kingdoms of men and gives them to anyone he wishes.' Immediately what had been said about Nebuchadnezzar was fulfilled. He was driven away from people and ate grass like cattle. His body was drenched with the dew of heaven until his hair grew like the feathers of an eagle and his nails like the claws of a bird. At the end of that time, I Nebuchadnezzar raised my eyes towards heaven and my sanity was restored. Then I praised the Most High; I honored and glorified him who lives forever."*

These scriptures were fulfilled in a literal manner. King Nebuchadnezzar lived in the wild much like an animal until he accepted and praised God. At that time, according to Daniel 4:36, his sanity was immediately restored and he subsequently recognized and glorified God.

Chapter 5: This chapter describes King Belshazzar (he is called the "son" of King Nebuchadnezzar., but the Aramaic term could mean "grandson" or even "successor"). King Belshazzar had a banquet using the gold and silver goblets that had been taken from the temple in Jerusalem. As they drank from these stolen goblets, suddenly the fingers of a human hand appeared and wrote on the plaster of the wall. The king called for the usual "enchanters and astrologers" to read the writing, but none could. Daniel again was brought in for the interpretation, which is given in **Daniel 5:18-30.** Daniel's interpretation of this writing was that God had "numbered the days" of King Belshazzar's reign, and "brought it to an end". He further stated that this kingdom would be divided and given to the Medes and Persians (consistent with the dream of Daniel 2 and the vision of Daniel 7) – which is exactly what happened. Daniel 5: 30 concludes the chapter: *"That very night Belshazzar, king of* *the Babylonians was slain and Darius the Mede took over the kingdom, at the age of sixty-two."* Again, this scripture reveals literal fulfillment of prophecy.

Chapter 6: In this chapter Daniel was "set-up" by the jealous royal administrators. They set up a decree that the king would issue, stating that anyone who prays to any God during the next 30 days (i.e., any God other than the king) would be thrown into the Lions Den. Daniel was caught praying and subsequently thrown into the den of Lions. Then, as stated by Daniel, in Daniel 6: 22, *"My God has sent his angels and he shut the mouths of the lions. They have not hurt me, because I was found innocent in his sight."* Daniel was completely unharmed despite having spent the night in this lion's den.

Chapter 7: This chapter describes a dream of Daniel's, which gives the exact same information as the dream of King Nebuchadnezzar in Chapter 2, but in a different way. The dream again details the same four successive gentile world kingdoms, or world empires, from the time of Daniel until the time of the Second Coming of Christ. In this dream, Daniel sees four beasts: The first like a **lion** (Babylonian Empire), the second beast was a **bear** (Mede-Persia Empire), the third, a **leopard** (Greece)**,** and the fourth beast (Roman Empire). This fourth beast was described as **"terrible and frightening and very powerful"** with "large iron teeth; it crushed and devoured its victims and trampled underfoot whatever was left. *"It was different from all the other beasts and it had ten horns. While I was thinking about the horns, there was before me another horn, a little one, which came up among them....This horn had eyes like the eyes of a man and a mouth that spoke boastfully."* This dream is interpreted in Daniel 7:17-27, starting with verse 17: *"The four great beasts are four kingdoms that* *will rise from the earth.*"

Chapter 7 elaborates on the fourth empire; the Roman Empire and Chapter 9 will give even greater detail regarding this final world empire. The book of Revelation will also explain and elaborate upon this final "revived" Roman Empire. Interestingly, Chapter 8 is where we receive detailed information on the second and third successive world empires (from the time of Daniel), the Medo-Persian Empire and the Greek Empire, thus confirming those two prophecies as literal fulfillment.

Daniel 7:19-20: *"Then I wanted to know about the fourth beast, which was different from all the others and the most terrifying, with its iron teeth and bronze claws...I also wanted to know about the ten horns on its head and about the other horn that came up, before which three of them fell – the horn that looked more imposing than the others and had eyes and a mouth that spoke boastfully"*.

Daniel 7:23-27 scriptures give a detailed explanation of the vision as described to Daniel by an angel. *"He gave me this explanation: 'The fourth beast is a fourth kingdom that will appear on earth. It will be different from all other kingdoms and will devour the whole earth, trampling it down and crushing it. **The ten horns are ten kings who will come from this kingdom. After them another king will arise, different from the earlier ones; he will subdue three kings. He will speak against the Most High and oppress his saints and try to change the set times and the laws. The saints will be handed over to him for a time, times and a half a time. But the court will sit, and his power will be taken away and completely destroyed forever. Then the sovereignty, power and greatness of the kingdoms will be handed over to the saints, and the people of the Most High. His kingdom will be an everlasting kingdom, and all rulers***

will worship and obey him.'"

Again, we see the imagery of "ten kings" which indicates either ten individual rulers or perhaps ten countries, or even ten regions of the world, with its leaders who will exist solely to support the Antichrist. This passage also reveals that for three and one-half years, intense persecution will take place, *"He will speak against the Most High and oppress his saints."* This passage also gives the exact same information as given in Daniel 2:44-45 in terms of describing the end of the reign of the Antichrist, *"His power will be taken away and completely destroyed forever."*

Daniel also reveals important additional details regarding this ruling body in Daniel 7:8: *"While I was thinking about the horns, there before me was another horn, a little one, which came up among them; and three of the first horns were uprooted before it."* This "little horn" represents the Antichrist, and the fact that he will arise from one of the countries of the revived Roman Empire which appears to be the current EU.

Further information on these three horns is mentioned in Daniel 7:24, *"...After them another king will arise, different from the earlier ones; he will subdue three kings."*

Daniel makes it clear that somehow three of the ten kings will be "uprooted" and "subdued" by the Antichrist. It is unclear exactly how or why this will happen, but presumably three of the "kings" will oppose the Antichrist in some way, leading to their being "uprooted."

{Footnote: The meaning of "time, times and half a time" is given in Revelation 12:6 and 12:14, where the same description of these "times" is given. Here, a description is given of "the woman", who represents Israel, during the last half of the tribulation, fleeing to the desert. In Revelation 12:6, we see that Israel must flee for 1,260 days. This information is repeated in Revelation 12:14, only here this same time period is given as "time, times and half a time". These two verses, taken together, tell us that this "time, times and half a time" means 1,260 days, or three and one-half years. Thus, "time" would mean one year, "times" would mean two years and "half a time" would be one-half of a year.}

To summarize these scriptures one can see the following: The last world empire will represent a "revival" of the original Roman Empire. We know this from Daniel 2 and Daniel 7, because the interpretation of these dreams/visions informs the reader that the Roman Empire will be in existence both at the time of Christ, beginning in 63 B.C., yet it will also be in existence during the Second Coming of Christ because Christ will end this final empire. Therefore, there must be a revival of this Roman Empire, in order for it to be in power at the time of the Second Coming. When a revival of this original Roman Empire is formed, it will consist of "ten kings" and this world empire will be different from all previous empires because it will "devour the whole earth, trampling it down and crushing it". The role of the ten kings will be to fully support a single ruler – the one "king" who will arise from these "10 kings" (verse 24) and he will speak out against Christ (verse 25) and he will persecute Christians (verse 25) during the seven year Tribulation. He will also put to death anyone who refuses to worship him as God. But at the Second Coming, he will lose his power, and he and his kingdom will be destroyed forever (Daniel 7:25-26 and Daniel 2:44-45) by Christ. This all occurs just prior to the Second Coming of Jesus.

The "ten horns" from Chapter 7 and the "ten toes" from Chapter 2 both represent the "ten kings" who will support and rule with the Antichrist. He will speak blasphemous words and oppose anything related to Christ. More detail on this Antichrist will follow in Daniel 9, and in Revelation 13.

His world domination, in concert with the "ten kings" who serve under him is also described in Revelation 12:3, 13:1, 17:3, and 17:9-14, giving us a full picture of this future prophecy.

Connections between Daniel and Revelation

Both Daniel and Revelation contain scriptures that describe the Tribulation, the Antichrist, the revived Roman Empire and its ten kings. In several instances, the passages in Revelation clarify and elaborate on information provided in the book of Daniel. There are several scriptural references to the "beast", each of which gives additional information. By combining the scriptures in Daniel and Revelation one can gain a full understanding of significant events and characters from the Tribulation.

Just as seen in Daniel 7:20-24, where the "beast" was described as having ten horns, the same ten horns are seen on the beast from Revelation 13:1, *"And I saw a beast coming out of the sea. He had ten horns and seven heads with ten crowns on his horns, and each one had a blasphemous name."* A very similar description of the beast was given in Revelation 12:3; *"an enormous red dragon with seven heads and ten horns and seven crowns on his heads."* The "crowns" simply represent rule/power/authority, thus we can see that both the ten horns (same "horns" as described in Daniel) and the seven heads represent ruling authority. Finally, Revelation 12:9 defines this dragon:

"The great dragon was hurled down – that ancient serpent called the devil, or Satan, who leads the whole world astray." From this verse it becomes clear that Satan will be working behind the scenes and influencing the Antichrist and the ten kings of the Tribulation.

A third passage describes this beast, as seen in

Revelation 17:3: *"...There I saw a woman sitting on a scarlet beast that was covered with blasphemous names and has 7 heads and 10 horns."* Again, here we see the exact same description of the beast with the seven heads and ten horns as given previously in Revelation 12 and 13. A detailed description also follows in Revelation 17:9-10 and 12-14:

"This calls for a mind with wisdom. The seven heads are seven hills on which the woman sits. There are also seven kings. Five have fallen, one is, the other has not yet come; but when he does come, he must remain for a little while. The ten horns you saw are ten kings (recall Daniel 7:24) *who have not yet received a kingdom, but who, for one hour will receive authority as kings along with the beast. They have one purpose and will give their power and authority to the beast. They will make war against the Lamb, but the Lamb will overcome them..."*

In these related passages from the book of Revelation, we receive detailed information on these seven world empires as they existed throughout history. Recall the four world empires as seen by Daniel: Babylon, Medo-Persia, Greece, and then Rome/Revived Rome. It is important to understand that Daniel's prophecy was looking forward from his perspective in time; the past was ignored in Daniel's prophecy. Now, in Revelation we get the same concept of gentile world kingdoms, only now the description of these world empires includes those which existed **prior to Daniel.** The explanation of these seven world empires is found in Revelation 17:10:

"There are also seven kings. Five have fallen, one is and the other has not yet come; but when he does he must remain for a little while."

The two gentile world kingdoms that existed prior to Daniel's life are now included: Egypt and Assyria. Recall that Egypt enslaved the Jews during the time of Moses, and the Assyrians conquered Israel in 722 B.C. Thus, the "five" that "have fallen" include all world empires throughout history all **prior to John's writing Revelation, including the two which existed prior to Daniel's writing:** Egypt, Assyria, Babylon, Medo-Persia, and Greece. Continuing in this passage, **"one is"** refers to the kingdom at the time of John's writing Revelation; the Roman Empire which existed at that time in history.

The final part of this description of gentile kingdoms throughout history reveals *"the other has not yet come, but when he does he must remain for a little while."* Note that this future world empire is referred to as "he", representing the Antichrist who will rule the world at some time in the future. We will learn in Daniel 9 that this "little while" will be a seven year period. The seven heads of this beast have now been explained in clear terms.

By continuing in this passage, we also receive an explanation of the ten horns. From Daniel, we know that the ten horns represent ten kings who will rule during the final world-ruling gentile kingdom. Revelation gives receive detailed information on this last kingdom or *"the other has not yet come."* Revelation 17:12 supports the text from Daniel:

"The ten horns you saw are ten kings who have not yet received a kingdom, but who, for one hour will receive authority as kings along with the beast." This verse represents the fact that the final ruling empire - a revival of the original Roman Empire - will be ruled by "ten kings". The "one hour" simply refers to a brief period of time. These ten kings will, in turn, be dominated and ruled by the Antichrist.

In summary, this connection between Revelation and Daniel give us two important elements for our understanding of this prophecy. The first is a chronological summary of gentile world empires or kingdoms as they existed throughout history. Each of these world empires had a direct influence upon the nation of Israel. Chronologically, these empires consisted of Egypt, Assyria, Babylon, Medo-Persia, Greece and Rome. Rome was ruling at the time of John's writing of Revelation. The second element is a detailed description of the final, remaining gentile kingdom, which is "yet to come". This world-ruling body will be characterized by ten "kings", and one individual "king" will arise from this revived Roman Empire who will gain absolute authority. Additionally this last "king", also known as the Antichrist will make war against Jesus ("the Lamb"), blaspheme God, persecute the Christians, and rule the entire world during the seven year period known as the Tribulation. A description of seven heads (representing the seven world-empires) and ten horns (representing the last world empire) are given as part of the "dragon". From Revelation 12:9, we know that Satan has had and will have a direct influence on all of these governments.

Chapter 8: This chapter describes Daniel's vision of a Ram and a Goat, which contains detailed information of the combined Mede-Persian Empire, followed by the Greek Empire which followed. This covered the second and third world empires taking place between 538 B.C. – 63 B.C., and confirmed the meaning of the chronological listing of the world empires given in Daniel 2 and 7.

Many scholars believe that Daniel 8:23-26 gives a brief description of the coming Antichrist. Daniel 8:23-26: *"In the latter part of their reign, when the rebels have become completely wicked, a stern-faced king, a master of intrigue, will arise. He will cause astounding devastation and will succeed in whatever he does. He will destroy the mighty men and the holy people. He will cause deceit to prosper, and he will consider himself superior. When they feel secure, he will destroy many and take his stand against the Prince of princes. Yet he will be destroyed, but not by human power."*

There are several good reasons to concur with the idea that these scriptures reference the fate of the Antichrist. First, the description references Christ as the "Prince of princes", who will be opposed by the Antichrist *"...and take his stand against the Prince of princes"* – a reference to the events at the Second Coming. Secondly, this passage describes the destruction of the Antichrist by non-human hands, an event that will only occur at the Second Coming when Christ destroys the Antichrist. This description parallels Daniel 2:42-45 and Daniel 7:26-27 – which are specific descriptions of Christ destroying the Antichrist and his unholy reign at the Second Coming. The phrase "when they feel secure" points to the period of peace that the Antichrist appears to bring to the world during the early part of his reign.

Chapter 9: This chapter gives us the "70 weeks" of Israel, which is God's time clock for Israel's history, past and future. This chapter also contains a basic framework of the overall prophecy for Israel. We also gain greater under-standing about the Antichrist and his actions during the final seven years of this "70 weeks".

The first verses of Daniel 9 are interesting because here, Daniel actually mentions the prophecy which had been given by Jeremiah years earlier. Jeremiah had predicted that the "desolation of Jerusalem", or the captivity of Jews into Babylon would last 70 years, and it lasted exactly 70 years. This scripture represents another literal fulfillment of prophecy.

Starting with Daniel 9:20, we see that the angel Gabriel appears to Daniel, *"Daniel I have now come to give you insight and understanding...Therefore consider the message and understand the vision."*

Daniel 9:24 contains a description of the purpose of the overall period of time given for the nation of Israel: *"Seventy 'weeks' are decreed for your people and your holy city to finish transgression, to put an end to sin, to atone for wickedness, to bring in everlasting righteousness, to seal up vision and prophecy and to anoint the most holy."*

The first question from the verse above is the meaning of the "week". Technically, from other parts of the Bible and from historical president a "week" represents a unit of 7 years (taken from Hebrew "shavuah" and Greek "heptad"). We also know from Genesis 29:27 that this period of a "week" represents seven years (this was Jacob's seven years of service in order to obtain Rachael). Thus, the "seventy weeks" or "seventy sevens", means 70, seven year periods which totals 490 years (7 x 70 = 490). From **Daniel 9:24** we know the following about this 490 year period which concludes at the end of the seven year tribulation period:

- The overall purpose: to fulfill the covenants with Israel
- To end Israel's failure ("transgression") to live under the law
- To make final atonement of sin
- To achieve reconciliation with God
- To establish a kingdom of everlasting righteousness
- To seal/complete prophecy
- To anoint the "most holy" – a reference to Christ's return

Daniel's Timeline

The beginning of this 490 year period is given in **Daniel 9:25, "Know and understand this: From the issuing of the decree to restore and rebuild Jerusalem until the Anointed One, the ruler comes, there will be seven "sevens", and 62** *"sevens"*. The Jewish time schedule is precise, unlike the "time of the gentiles" which has no set time period given. Its purpose is to give specific periods of time for various events, thus fulfilling prophecy in a precise and literal manner. Additionally, the time would have a specific, designated starting point and ending point, and by doing so the projected time periods would not be in doubt.

The "starting point" of Daniel's timeline was clearly given as *"the issuing of a decree to restore and rebuild Jerusalem."* This refers to the decree of the Persian emperor Artaxerxes Longimanus, who sent Nehemiah to Jerusalem specifically to rebuild the city wall (Nehemiah 2:1-6). This was a memorable date because it marked the beginning of the long process of rebuilding and it gave Jerusalem independence and protection against invasions of their neighbors. Nehemiah's record is precise, and the decree was given in 445 B.C.

To continue with this scripture and to understand the first two time-periods we read the rest of Daniel 9:25, *"...until the Anointed One, the ruler comes, there will be seven "sevens" and 62 "sevens".* We see this 483 period (69 'weeks') broken up into two parts. The first period was given as 49 years, or 7 "sevens". This 49 year period coincides with the completion of the rebuilding of Jerusalem. Interestingly, this period also saw the conclusion of the time of the Old Testament prophets (which started the 400 years of prophetic "silence" which remained until the emergence of John the Baptist). The second of these time periods, the 62 remaining weeks will conclude when *"the Anointed One, the ruler comes"*. By adding the two consecutive time periods given (i.e. adding 7 "sevens" to 62 "sevens"), we get a total period of 69 "sevens" which equals 483 years. This period began in 445 B.C. – with the "decree" given to Nehemiah to rebuild Jerusalem.

In 32 A.D, on Palm Sunday – Jesus entered Jerusalem as

"the King who comes in the name of the Lord" (Psalm 118:26 and Luke 19:38). The prophet Zechariah (Zechariah 9:9) revealed this to be the day *"your King is coming to you....riding on a donkey."* This date marks the ending of this 483 year period. By calculating the number of days, beginning at the decree given to Nehemiah and ending with Jesus entering Jerusalem as the Messiah, the exact period of time is indeed 483 years, just as the angel Gabriel informed Daniel (2). Once again, the prophecies are fulfilled in a literal way.

Israel's Clock Stops During the Church Age

From the scriptures we can see that after the conclusion of this 483 year period (69 "sevens"), there are at least two specific events that take place before the concluding last "seven", or last seven year period begins. These two events, because they are not given as part of the overall 70 'week' time period indicate that there is a "gap" between the 69th and 70th weeks. The Jewish timeclock stopped when the Messiah was "cut off". This "gap" in time between the 69th and 70th "seven" represents the "Church Age".

The scripture reveals this point in Daniel 9:26:

"After the sixty-two 'sevens', the Anointed One will be cut off and will have nothing. The people of the ruler who will come will destroy the city and the sanctuary."

We can see that the first event occurring after the 69th 'week' concluded: The crucifixion of Jesus ("the Anointed One will be cut off"). The second event given in this scripture described the destruction of Jerusalem ("destroy the city and sanctuary"). This destruction of Jerusalem occurred in the aftermath of a Jewish revolt and the subsequent siege of the city by the Romans in 70 A.D., just as Jesus predicted in Matthew 24. Both events took place after the 69th week, but were not part of the last seven year period.

The fact that these two enormously important events are given in Daniel 9:26, as occurring **before** the description of the final seven years clearly indicates a gap in the timeclock for Israel's people. The fact that this gap exists is further confirmed by Jesus' discussion of end times (Matthew 24:15), where he stated that the "abomination of desolation" (a description of the Antichrist declaring himself as God) would not occur until shortly before his Second Coming. For this prophecy he had to assume that a gap would exist between the 69th and 70th weeks. We also know that this "gap" in time exists simply because the detailed events of the final 7 years have not yet occurred. Importantly the "Church Age", which is the defining event during this "gap", must also be concluded before God turns his attention back to the nation of Israel.

The Last "Week" of Daniel's Timeline: The Tribulation

Daniel's prophecy tells us the relative timing of the last seven year period in Daniel 9: 27:

"He will confirm a covenant with many for one 'seven'. In the middle of the 'seven' he will put an end to sacrifice and offering. And on a wing of the temple he will set up an abomination that causes desolation, until the end that is decreed, is poured out on him."

In this passage, we receive additional information regarding the Antichrist. In verse 26 above, we can see an interesting fact about the Antichrist: *"The people of the ruler who will come will destroy the city and the sanctuary."* We know from history that the Romans destroyed Jerusalem in 70 A.D. Therefore, the Romans are "the people" referred to in this scripture. This "ruler", or the Antichrist, is identified as someone who comes from the same origin as these Romans, thus, he will emerge from one of the countries which formed the Roman Empire. This is fully consistent with Daniel 2, Daniel 7 and Revelation 17.

We also see that he will *"confirm a covenant"* for one *"seven"*, which represents this last seven year period. The scripture informs us that he is the same person identified in **Daniel 7:24** (a king arising from the ten "horns" or ten "kings"), in **Revelation 17:9-14** and described by Jesus in **Matthew 24:15-16**. This important phrase *"He will confirm a covenant with many for a week"* tells us that this significant event – the confirming of the covenant – will mark the beginning of the last seven year period as given to Daniel by the angel Gabriel. This is also known as the "Tribulation" which is described by Jesus, in the Olivet Discourse (Matthew 24/25), by Paul (2 Thessalonians 2:1-1), and by John (Revelation 6-19).

Other important facts arise from this passage; 1) the temple has been rebuilt since this is where the "abomination of desolation" takes place. The "abomination of desolation" takes place at the mid-point of this seven year period, thus, sometime prior to this, the temple must be re-built, 2) the Antichrist will put an end to sacrifice, thus we assume that at some point during the last seven years, animal sacrifice will begin again in the temple. Interestingly, this final seven year period seems to pick up exactly where the clock "stopped", at the time of Christ's death.

False Peace

This "covenant" will confirm a peace treaty between Israel and the surrounding countries, and those in power to enforce such a treaty, thus the meaning of "the many". It is felt to be a peace treaty, as the Antichrist will appear to bring peace at the beginning of his rise to power. These ideas are consistent with Daniel 8:25, *"He will cause deceit to prosper and he will consider himself superior. When they feel secure, he will destroy many and take his stand against the Prince of princes. Yet he will be destroyed, but not by human power."* This is a reference to the Antichrist causing deceit to prosper (initially) and later destroying "many" through warfare and persecution. However, he will be destroyed by Christ at the time of the Second Coming.

We also find related information in 1 Thessalonians 5:2: *"for you know very well that the day of the Lord will come like a thief in the night. While people are saying 'Peace and safety', destruction will come on them suddenly, as labor pains on a pains on a pregnant woman, and they will not escape."* This verse adds more detail regarding the false peace that the Antichrist will appear to create.

Revelation also reveals this initial appearance of peace with the symbolism of the first horseman, which is also the first "seal judgment" of the Tribulation in Revelation 6:1-2: *"I looked, and there before me was a white horse! Its rider held a bow, and he was given a crown, and he rode out as a conqueror bent on conquest..."* This first horseman reveals a rider with a crown, indicating authority, and a bow without arrows, suggesting that he conquers the world via peace as opposed to warfare. It appears from these passages that, at least in the initial part of the Tribulation, the Antichrist will appear to be creating peace in the Middle East.

The Abomination

Following these events (signing of the covenant, animal sacrifices, rebuilding of the temple, etc.), we see in Daniel 9:27 *"In the middle of the 'week' he will put an end to sacrifice and offering. And on a wing of the temple he will set up an abomination that causes desolation, until the end that is decreed..."* This was the exact reference that Jesus warned about in Matthew 24:15, *"So when you see standing in the holy place 'the abomination of desolation' spoken of through the prophet Daniel – let the reader understand – then let those who are in Judea flee to the mountains."* At this point, the half-way point into the seven year Tribulation, the Antichrist will break his covenant with Israel and desecrate the temple by proclaiming himself as God. This will begin a period known as the "Great Tribulation", a period in which Jesus warned the Jews to flee. This period will involve intense persecution/holocaust of the Jews, and is described in detail in the book of Revelation.

Summary

In summary, the book of Daniel gives an outline of significant world events occurring from the sixth century B.C. until the Second Coming of Christ. In Daniel we see the various gentile kingdoms that play an important part in world history, particularly as they exerted great influence over the nation of Israel. The greatest emphasis is placed upon the last gentile kingdom. By the explanations given in Daniel and further clarification in the appropriate parts of Revelation, we see that that the last world empire will look like a revival of the ancient Roman Empire and it will include "ten kings", presumably representing ten countries or the individuals ruling over ten countries or perhaps ten regions of the world. These "ten kings" will support a ruler who emerges from this revived Roman Empire. The ruler will "confirm" a peace covenant between Israel and "the many" (presumably the surrounding countries with whom Israel has been having conflict), and this covenant will allow: 1) the temple to be rebuilt, and 2) for the Jews to resume animal sacrifices, thus instituting Israel's old ritual system. One can see that the temple must be re-built on the original site of the old Temple Mount in order for the sacrificial system to be carried out. The confirmation of this apparent peace covenant will signal the beginning of the last seven years of Daniel's "70 weeks", or also known as the Tribulation.

Currently, the Muslim's Dome of the Rock occupies this site where the temple belongs. Obviously the Muslims would not allow this re-building of the temple on that site. For this reason it is assumed that the "covenant" the Antichrist confirms will consist of some sort of peace agreement and/or an agreement which allow various concessions between the Jews and the Muslims allowing for the temple rebuilding. Following these events, the "peace" covenant will be broken by the Antichrist, signaled by the "abomination of desolation" which indicates the Antichrist proclaiming himself as God from the temple.

With this signal, Jesus warned the people in Jerusalem at that time to flee, as both persecution and judgments upon the earth will peak during the next three and one-half years. However, this period will end with Jesus Second Coming and the subsequent defeat of the Antichrist.

Daniel's timeline can be summarized as below:

The 70 Weeks of Daniel

[——————————70 "weeks", or 490 years——————]
[—— 483 years————*]—**Church Age**—[**—7 years—]

*Jesus enters Jerusalem on Palm Sunday
** Antichrist "confirms" the covenant with Israel

Chapter 12: Chapter 12 contains two interesting points: 1)

Daniel 12:4, *"but you, Daniel, close up and seal the words of the scroll until the time of the end"* and Daniel 12:9, *"Go your way Daniel, because the words are closed up and sealed until the time of the end."* This indicates that the words of prophecy were complete in this book, and should remain unaltered until the time of their fulfillment. It has only been in the last 20-30 years that detailed analyses, publication and popularity about these prophecies, along with other pertinent biblical scriptures, has taken place. This resurgence in Bible prophecy interest indicates these scriptures as now being "unsealed", 2) Daniel 12:4, *"...Many will go here and there, and knowledge shall increase."* This verse can be interpreted as widespread travel meaning to literally "go here and there" physically or "travel to and fro" intellectually, indicating a significant increase in knowledge. As with many prophecies, it could have a duel meaning referencing both widespread knowledge and travel. The last century has witnessed an explosion in knowledge and technology, incomparable to any other generation in the history of the world. One key to these scriptures in Chapter 12 is the message that Daniel will not be analyzed on a broad, public scale until the "time of the end". The very fact that these scriptures, for the first time in history are being widely published, read and understood in a literal way gives yet another indication that we are indeed living in the latter days.

CHAPTER SEVEN NOTES

1. Dwight Pentecost. Prophecy for Today. God's Purpose and Plan for Our Future (Zondervan Publishing House. 1961).
2. John F Walvoord. Daniel: The Key to Prophetic Revelation. A Commentary by John F. Walvoord (Moody Press. 1971).

EIGHT

THE ANTICHRIST

Revelation 13:7: He was given power to make war against the saints and to conquer them. And he was given authority over every tribe, people, language and nation.

Daniel 7:26: But the court will sit, and his power will be taken away and completely destroyed forever.

The individual commonly referred to as the Antichrist is known by several names throughout the Bible, with each description giving aspects of his nature: **"Man of lawlessness"** (2 Thessalonians 2:3), **"lawless one"** (2 Thessalonians 2:8), **"little horn"** (Daniel 7:8), **"ruler that shall come"** (Daniel 9:26), and **"the beast"** (Revelation 13:5). The actual term **"Antichrist"** is given to us by John in 1 John 2:18 and 2 John 1:7. The prefix "anti" indicates that he is both "against" Christ (in opposition of Christ) and will also show himself to be a "false" Christ as Jesus warned about in Matthew 24:23.

The Antichrist will rule the final World Empire, which will consist of a revival of the old "Roman Empire", and his reign will take place during the seven year Tribulation. Initially he will appear to be a peace-maker (1 Thessalonians 5:2-3; Revelation 6: 2; Daniel 8:25). At the midpoint of the Tribulation, the Antichrist will proclaim himself as God, from the rebuilt temple, and at this point will inflict severe persecution upon both Christians and Jews who do not worship him as God (Daniel 7:21, 7:25 and 9:27; Matthew 24:15; Revelation 13:7). People will be forced to worship him or face death (Revelation13:8 and 13:14-15). He will force people to take "the Mark of the Beast" in order to be able to "buy or sell", or to complete any financial transaction (Revelation 13:16-17). He will blaspheme God (Daniel 7:25; Revelation 13:5-6). He will gather together the armies of the world at "Armageddon" (the valley of Megiddo) by deception (Revelation 16:13-16, 19:19) in order to ultimately make war with Christ (Revelation 19:19). He will be struck down by Christ at the time of the Second Coming (Revelation 19:20; Daniel7:26).

There are at least 15 defining characteristics of the Antichrist which are unique to the Antichrist and only one person will fit all of these criteria:

1. He will rise to power in the last days, just before the second coming of Christ (Daniel 7:26-27, 9:27; Matthew 24: 29-30)
2. He will not be identified as the Antichrist until after the Rapture occurs (2 Thessalonians 2:6-8).
3. He will rule "every tribe, people, language and nation" (Revelation 13:7).
4. He will rule by international consent (Revelation 17:12-13).
5. He will rule by deception (Daniel 8:24-25; 2 Thessalonians. 2:9-11).
6. He will display "counterfeit miracles, signs and wonders" (2 Thessalonians 2:9-10).
7. He will be "strong", "imposing" and "boastful" (Daniel 7:20, 8:24-25, Revelation 13:5).
8. He will be assisted by a "False Prophet" (Revelation 13:11-18).

9. He and the False Prophet will control the global economy by implementing the "Mark of the Beast" (Revelation 13:16-17).
10. He will make, and then break a covenant with Israel (Daniel 9:26-27).
11. He will claim to be God (2 Thessalonians 2:4, Matthew 24:15 and Daniel 9:27).
12. He will institute intense persecution of Jews and Christians (Daniel 7:21; Matthew 24:15-22; Revelation 13:7).
13. There will be forced worship of the Antichrist and an "image" of the Antichrist and refusal to do so will result in death (Revelation 13:8, 13:14-15).
14. He will gather the armies of the world together at "Armageddon" (the valley of Megiddo) just before the second coming of Christ (Revelation 16:13-16, 19:19).
15. His reign will be ended by Christ at the time of the Second Coming and he will be thrown into the "lake of fire" (2 Thessalonians 2:8, Daniel 2:44, 7:26; Revelation 19:20-21).

Scriptural References Describing the Antichrist

• **"Man of Sin" – 2 Thessalonians 2:3:** *"Let no man deceive you by any means for that day shall not come, except there come a falling away first, and that man of sin be revealed, the son of perdition" (KJV).* This description is part of the overall passage describing the fact that (according to the original meaning) the Antichrist will not be revealed until after the "falling away" or (as seen in earlier translations), after the "departure" occurs. There are two schools of thought regarding the meaning of "falling away" or "departure".

This is often considered to be either a reference to end times apostasy ("falling away") or it may also serve as a reference to the Rapture ("departure"). Importantly, we see this reference of the "man of sin" emerging onto the world scene – this emergence will signal the beginning reign of the Antichrist.

- **"Lawless One"** – **2 Thessalonians 2:8:** *"And then the **lawless one** will be revealed, whom the Lord Jesus will overthrow with the breath of his mouth and destroy with the splendor of his coming."* This is part of the description involving the fact that the Church will be raptured before the Antichrist can be revealed.

- **"Little Horn"** – **Daniel 7:8:** *"While I was thinking about the horns, there before me was another horn, a little one which came up among them...**This horn had eyes like the eyes of a man, and a mouth that spoke boastfully**."* This passage comes from the detailed description of the last gentile kingdom, in the context of the Antichrist rising from these ten kings for the purpose of his world rule.

- **"The ruler who will come"** – **Daniel 9:26:** *"The people of the ruler who will come will destroy the city and the sanctuary."* This passage is part of the description of the two events occurring between Daniel's 69th and 70th weeks; specifically, the destruction of Jerusalem and the temple. What this verse is saying, is that the "ruler", or the Antichrist, will come from one of the countries which forms the Roman Empire.

- **"The beast"** – **Revelation 13:5:** *"**The beast** was given a mouth to utter proud words and blasphemies and to exercise his authority for forty-two months."* Chapter 13 of the book of Revelation gives one of the most detailed descriptions of the Antichrist. This passage describes his use of blasphemy – perhaps driven, at least partially by his enormous ego.

- **"Peace and safety" – 1 Thessalonians 5:3:** *"While people are saying 'Peace and safety', destruction will come on them suddenly, as labor pains on a pregnant woman, and they will not escape."* The context for this scripture is set up in the preceding verse (1 Thessalonians 5:2), *"For you know very well that the day of the Lord will come like a thief in the night"*. The "day of the Lord" gives us the reference point, which is the Tribulation. Thus, what we see in this scripture is a reference to the first part of the Tribulation, in which the Antichrist appears to create "peace and safety", yet it will be a false peace, because soon after this sense of peace, the Antichrist will turn against the Christians and Jews (Matthew 24:15). At this point, Jesus informs his believers to flee because of the nature of this intense persecution. Similarly, **Revelation 6:2** gives us the same information, as seen by the representation of the Antichrist emerging as a rider on a white horse with a bow but no arrow, *"I looked, and there before me was a white horse! Its rider held a bow, and he was given a crown, and he rode out as a conqueror bent on conquest."* Here, the crown indicates authority and the bow, without arrows suggests that he conquers the world diplomatically, by the offer of peace (1). Further, we can see the similar descriptions from **Daniel 8:25**, *"He will cause deceit to prosper, and he will consider himself superior. **When they feel secure**, he will destroy many and take his stand against the Prince of princes. Yet he will be destroyed, but not by human power."*

- **"The abomination of desolation" - Daniel 9:27, Mathew 24:15-16:** *"He will confirm a covenant with the many for one 'seven'. In the middle of the 'seven' he will put an end to sacrifice and offering. And on a wing of the temple he will set up an abomination that causes desolation, until the end that is decreed is poured out on him."(Daniel 9:27), "So when you see standing in the holy place 'the abomination that causes desolation', spoken of through the prophet Daniel – let the reader understand – then let those who are in Judea flee to the mountains."(Matthew 24:15-16).* From these descriptions, we can see that in the middle of the seven year Tribulation, the Antichrist will proclaim himself as God; he will create an image representing him that people will be forced to worship. At that time, the believers living there ("those in Judea") have to flee in order to avoid the wrath of the Antichrist. This "abomination" causes "desolation"; desolation is defined as a feeling of despair; devastation; ruin; and laying waste to a place. The Antichrist causes this scenario due to this abomination created when he proclaimed himself as God.

- **Persecution – Daniel 7:21, Daniel 7:25 and Revelation 13:7:** *"As I watched, this horn was waging **war against the saints** and defeating them, until the Ancient of Days came and pronounced judgment in favor of the saints of the Most High, and the time came when they possessed the kingdom."(Daniel 7:21), "He will speak against the Most High and **oppress his saints...The saints will be handed over to him...**" (Dan. 7:25), "He was given power to **make war against the saints and to conquer them.**"(Revelation 13:7).* From these scriptures we can see that the Tribulation will involve intense persecution "of the saints"; the believers in Christ.

- **Forced Worship of the Antichrist – Revelation 13:8, 13:14-15:** *"All inhabitants of the earth will worship the beast – all whose names have not been written in the book of life belonging to the Lamb that was slain..."* (Revelation 13:8), *"He ordered them to set up an image of the beast...He was given power to give breath to the image of the first beast, so that it could speak and cause all who refused to worship the image to be killed."* (Revelation 13:14-15).

- **He will Control the Global Economy – Revelation 13:16-17:** *"He also forced everyone, small and great, rich and poor, free and slave, to receive a mark on his right hand or on his forehead, so that no one could buy or sell unless he had the mark..."* Technically, the "he" in the beginning of the scripture refers to the False Prophet, but his actions will be dictated by the Antichrist, and the Mark of the Beast will, in some way, represent loyalty to the Antichrist. One will not be able to buy or sell goods without this Mark of the Beast – thus, all believers who live during the Tribulation will have to find other means of gathering money and food. If one takes the Mark of the Beast, he/she will have clearly determined their alignment with the Antichrist and they will have determined their fate, *"If anyone worships the beast and his image **and receives his mark on the forehead or on the hand, he too will drink of the wine of God's fury.**"* (Revelation 14:9-10)

- **Blasphemy of God – Daniel 7:25 and Revelation 13:5-6:** *"He will speak against the Most High"* (Daniel 7:25), *"The beast was given a mouth to utter proud words and blasphemies and to exercise his authority for forty-two months. **He opened his mouth to blaspheme God, and to slander his name** and his dwelling place and those* *who live in heaven."*

- **He will Precipitate Armageddon – Revelation 16:13-16, 19:19:** *"Then I saw three evil spirits...they came out of the mouth of the dragon, out of the mouth of the beast and out of the mouth of the False Prophet. They are spirits of demons performing miraculous signs, and they go out to the kings of the whole world, **to gather them for the battle on the great day of God Almighty"***(Revelation 16:13-14). *"Then they gathered the kings together to **the place that in Hebrew is called Armageddon"*** (Revelation 16:16). *"Then I saw the beast and the kings of the earth and their armies gathered together to make war against the rider on the horse and his army."*(Revelation 19:19). These scriptures describe the Antichrist gathering his armies ultimately to make war against Christ, just as Christ makes his appearance at the time of the Second Coming. The description of Armageddon refers to the mount of Megiddo located next to the plain or valley of Megiddo. Megiddo is the Hebrew word corresponding to the Greek word Armageddon (2).

- **The Antichrist Rise to Power is in the Last Days – Daniel 7:26-27, 9:27, Matthew 24:29-30:** *"But the court will sit and his power will be taken away and completely destroyed forever. Then the sovereignty, power and greatness of the kingdoms under the whole heaven will be handed over to the saints, the people of the Most High"*(Daniel 7:26-27), and *"...he will set up an abomination that causes desolation, until the end that is decreed is poured out on him"* (Daniel 9:27). Here we can see that "the end that is decreed" refers to the end of the "seventieth week" of Daniel's timeline for the nation of Israel, which occurs at the time of the Second Coming of Jesus. The passage, *"Immediately after the distress of* *those days"* is a reference to the Tribulation, which leads to the following: *"At that time the sign of the Son of Man will appear in the sky...They will see the Son of Man coming on the clouds of the sky with power and great glory"* (Revelation 24:29-30). So what we can put together from these scriptures and from Matthew 24:13-30 is the overall flow of events, starting with the Antichrist proclamation that he is God (abomination of desolation) and ending with the return of Christ. From these passages, we can see that the time of the Antichrist's reign will begin at the signing of the peace covenant (Daniel 9:27) which begins the Tribulation, and will end at the Second Coming of Christ (Matthew 24:30, Revelation 19:19-21).

• **The "World-Rule" of the Antichrist – Revelation 13:7:** *"And he was given authority over every tribe, people, language and nation."*

• **The "World-Rule" will be Accepted by International Consent – Revelation 17:12-13:** *"The ten horns you saw are the ten kings who have not yet received a kingdom, but who for one hour will receive authority as kings along with the beast. **They have one purpose and will give their power and authority to the beast.**"*

• **He will Rule by Deception – Daniel 8:23-25 and 2 Thessalonians 2:9-11:** *"...a stern-faced king, a master of intrigue..."* (Daniel 8:23); *"He will cause **deceit to prosper** and he will consider himself superior"* (Daniel 8:25); *"The coming of the lawless one will be in accordance with the work of Satan displayed in all kinds of **counterfeit miracles, signs and wonders, and in every sort of evil that deceives**...For this reason God sends them a **powerful delusion** so that they will believe the* *lie...*" (2 Thessalonians 2:9-11).

- **He will be Strong, Imposing and Boastful – Daniel 7:
20, 8:24-25 and Revelation 13:5:** "*...the horn that
looked more imposing than the others and that had eyes
and a mouth that spoke boastfully*"(Daniel 7:20); "*He
will become very strong, but not by his own power...and
he will consider himself superior*" (Dan. 8:24-25); "*The
beast was given a mouth to utter **proud words** and **blasphemies** and to exercise his authority...*" (Revelation
13:5). By putting these scriptures together, it would
appear that the Antichrist will have an inflated self-
image and he will appear to most people an imposing,
strong, superior, boastful person who is consumed with
blasphemy and hatred of Christ.

- **He Declares Himself to be God – 2 Thessalonians 2:4:**
"*He will oppose and will exalt himself over everything
that is called God or is worshiped, so that he sets himself
up in God's temple, **proclaiming himself to be God.**"*

- **His Reign will be Ended by Christ – Revelation 19:20-
21, 2 Thessalonians 2:8:** "*But the beast was captured,
and with him the False Prophet who had preformed the
miraculous signs on his behalf. The two of them were
thrown alive into the fiery lake of burning sulfur.*"
(Revelation 19:20-21). "*And then the lawless one will be
revealed whom the Lord **Jesus will overthrow with the
breath of his mouth and destroy with the splendor of his
coming**"* (2 Thessalonians 2:8).

CHAPTER EIGHT NOTES

1. Tim LaHaye. Prophecy Study Bible (AMG Publishers. 2000).
2. John F. Walvoord. The Revelation of Jesus Christ. A Commentary by John F. Walvoord (Moody Press. 1981).

NINE

THE RAPTURE OF THE CHURCH

1 Thessalonians 4:16: For the Lord himself will come down from heaven with a loud command, with the voice of the archangel and with the trumpet call of God, and the dead in Christ will rise first. After that, we who are still alive will be caught up together with them in the clouds to meet the Lord in the air. And so we will be with the Lord forever.

John 14:1-3: Do not let your hearts be troubled. Trust in God; trust also in me. In my fathers house there are many rooms; if it were not so, I would have told you. I am going there to prepare a place for you. And if I go and prepare a place for you, I will come back and take you to be with me that you may also be where I am.

In 1 Corinthians 15:51, Paul introduces a new topic to the church *"Behold, I tell you a mystery"*. This "mystery" is described in greater detail in 1 and 2 Thessalonians. Paul gives us specific and detailed information regarding certain events which will occur at the end of the age. A literal interpretation of these events describes a Rapture of the Church followed at a later time by the Second Coming of Christ. The Rapture of the Church is defined as a return of Christ reserved exclusively for His Church (believers in Christ) in which He instantly removes all believers from earth – to meet Him in the air. These believers experience an instantaneous change in their bodies from an earthly body to a "heavenly body", and then are taken with Jesus to the "Father's house". These believers will not experience a physical death (1 Corinthians 15:51-54; 1 Thessalonians 4:15-18). A literal interpretation also details that this Rapture will occur before the beginning of the Tribulation, thus removing the Church from earth before this seven year period. The word "Rapture" comes from a Latin translation of the Greek word "harpazo" which means "to seize" or to "snatch away".

Interpretation of the Bible in a literal manner indicates that the Rapture is a distinct and separate event from the Second Coming. The various descriptions which are given in the scriptures as they relate to the Rapture are strikingly different as compared to the events describing the Second Coming. The distinctions between the events described by Paul (Rapture) and the events described for the Second Coming (Revelation, Matthew, and Zechariah) are clear. A literal interpretation of the pertinent scriptures reveals that Christ's return will occur in two stages – the first stage indicates that Christ will return "in the air" to take His people, the Church out of this world (Rapture) and later He will return "with his saints" to set up His 1,000 year kingdom on earth (Second Coming). Between these two stages the seven year Tribulation will occur.

Those who believe that the Rapture will take place before the beginning of the Tribulation are called "pre-Tribulationists" or believe in the "pre-Tribulation" Rapture. Those who believe that the Church will be raptured at the mid-point in the Tribulation are called "mid-Tribulationists", or they hold the "mid-Tribulation" view. This belief is focused on the Rapture as occurring prior to the last half-half of the Tribulation. There are also those who believe that the Rapture will occur at the very end of the Tribulation and are thus called "post-Tribulationists", as they believe in a "post-Tribulation" Rapture. The most literal translation of the scripture is a Rapture which occurs before the Tribulation, or points to a pre-Tribulation Rapture.

The Bride of Christ

One important aspect in terms of understanding the Rapture of the Church involves knowledge of the intimate relationship between Jesus and His Church (1, 2). This relationship, as described in multiple occasions, is seen as that of a bride and bridegroom:

The Church Represents the Bride of Jesus: This imagery represents a fundamental aspect for understanding various events of the Rapture and "the wedding" between Christ and the Church which will take place in Heaven during the Tribulation. There are several scriptural references which explain the image of "the Church" as representing the bride of Christ:

• **Ephesians 5:22-32**: *"Husbands, love our wives just as Christ loved the church and gave himself up for her to make her holy, cleansing her by the washing with water through the word and to present her to himself as a radiant church, without stain or wrinkle or any blemish, but holy and blameless......For this reason a man will leave his father and mother and become united to his wife, and the two will become one flesh. **This is a profound mystery-but I am talking about Christ and the church.**"* This scripture defines the relationship we, the Church have with Christ when filled with the Holy Spirit – we become one with Christ, just as a wife and husband become one. Paul further adds clarification that the "bride/bridegroom" relationship is the same as Christ

145

and the Church, *"I am talking about Christ and the Church."*

- **Matthew 9:14-15**: *"Then John's disciples came and asked him, 'How is it that we and the Pharisees fast, but your disciples do not fast?' Jesus answered 'How can the guests of the bridegroom mourn when he is with them? The time will come when the bridegroom will be taken from them; then they will fast.'"* In this passage, again, Christ defines himself as the bridegroom.

- **John 3:28-29**: Here, John the Baptist describes his role as supporting the bridegroom (Jesus), *"You yourselves can testify that I said, 'I am not the Christ but am sent ahead of him.' The bride belongs to the bridegroom. The friend who attends the bridegroom waits and listens for him, and is full of joy when he hears the bridegroom's voice."*

- **2 Corinthians 11:2**: *"...I promised you to one husband, to Christ, so that I might present you as a pure virgin."*

- **Revelation 19:7-9**: *"Let us rejoice and be glad and give him glory!* **For the wedding of the Lamb has come and the bride has made herself ready.** *Fine linen, bright and clean was given her to wear. Then the angel said to me, 'Write: Blessed are those who are invited to the wedding supper of the Lamb.' And he added, 'These are the true words of God.'"* Here, and similarly in Revelation 21:2, and Revelation 21:9 we also see the image of the relationship between the bridegroom (Jesus) and the bride (the Church) with the "wedding" having occurred in Heaven. From the flow of events given in the book of Revelation, it is apparent that this "wedding" took place in Heaven during the Tribulation. We are informed that the wedding has already taken place – before the Second Coming of Christ. This argues strongly against a post-Tribulation Rapture, as a post-Tribulation Rapture would not have allowed time for this "wedding" to take place.

Summary of Ancient Marriage Customs

1. The marriage contract or "betrothal" was agreed between the fathers of the future couple.
2. Once the couple reached the appropriate age for marriage, the groom traveled from his home to the prospective Bride's home to "pay the purchase price" thus establishing the covenant.
3. The groom returns to his father's house, and remains separate from the Bride while preparing living accommodations for his wife.
4. The groom returns for his bride at an unknown time.
5. His return with her to the groom's father's house to consummate the marriage, then to celebrate the wedding feast.

The Hebrew custom of the events of the marriage, vividly describe the events of the Rapture and then what takes place in Heaven between the "bride" (Church) and the "bridegroom" (Jesus). Below are the biblical events which correspond to the 5 main events in this marriage custom:

1. The "betrothal" of the believer to Christ took place before we were even born. Ephesians 1:4-5, *"For he chose us in him before the creation of the world to be holy and blameless in his sight. In love he predestined us to be adopted as his sons through Jesus Christ, in accordance with his pleasure and will."*

2. The "bridegroom", Jesus, leaves his "home" (heaven)

to come to earth (Bride's home) to "pay the purchase price" (die for our salvation), thus establishing the covenant. This dramatic event was confirmed on the cross.

3. The "bridegroom", Jesus, returns to his father's house (literally) and prepares living accommodations for his "bride" (the Church). John 14:3 confirms this fact: ***"Do not let your hearts be troubled. Trust in God; trust also in me. In my Father's house there are many rooms; if it were not so, I would have told you. I am going there to prepare a place for you. And if I go and prepare a place for you, I will come back and take you to be with me so that you may also be where I am."*** Also noteworthy here, is the fact that this description does not fit with the description of the Second Coming, because the Second Coming will involve Christ coming **with** His Church to earth, not **taking** His Church/bride to his father's house. Additionally, at the Second Coming, Christ will remain on earth for 1,000 years and is not taking His Church anywhere at that point.

4. The "bridegroom", Jesus, returns for His bride (the Church), **at an unknown time.** This is bolded because it represents one important distinction between the Second Coming and the Rapture. The Second Coming will occur immediately after the end of the seven year tribulation period (Matthew 24:29, Daniel 9:27) and three and one-half years after "The Abomination of Desolation" takes place (Daniel 9:27, Matthew 24:15-25, 2 Thessalonians 2:4). Exactly 1,260 days will transpire from this mid-point of the Tribulation until the Second Coming of Christ (Revelation 12:6 and 13:4). Both of these events (the

beginning of the Tribulation and the mid-point in the Tribulation) will occur at identifiable dates, thus allowing one to calculate the time of the Second Coming. The Rapture, however takes place at an unknown time (Matthew 24:36, 24:44, 25:13; Revelation 3: 3), just as described.

5. After Jesus comes for his Church or "bride", then He will take these believers to His fathers house (John 14: 1-3).

The Events of the Rapture

• The Lord will descend from heaven, with a "loud command" (1 Thessalonians 4:16).

• He will come again to receive us to Himself and take us to a place which He has prepared for each of us (John 14:1-3).

• We will hear the voice of an archangel (possibly to lead Israel during the Tribulation; 1 Thessalonians 4:16).

• We will also hear the trumpet call of God (1 Thessalonians 4:16).

• The dead in Christ (those who have died during the Church Age) will rise first (1 Thessalonians 4:16-17, 1 Corinthians 15:52). The corruptible ashes of their dead bodies are made incorruptible and joined together with their spirit.

• Then, we who are alive and remain shall be changed and made incorruptible by having our bodies made "immortal"

(1 Corinthians 15:51, 53:1 and Thessalonians 4:17).

• Then we shall be caught up, "in the clouds" to meet the Lord "in the air", and we shall "ever be with the Lord" in Heaven (1 Thessalonians 4:17 and John 14:1-3).

• The judgment seat of Christ (the "bema" judgment), which is not a judgment that determines salvation, but a review of works and for rewards therein. This event is for "judgment" of things done while in the body (2 Corinthians 5:10 and 3:11-15). The various "crowns" for certain acts will be recognized and rewarded (1 Corinthians 9:25; Revelation 2:10; 1 Peter 5:2-4; 2 Timothy 4:8 and 1 Thessalonians 2:19-20).

• The marriage of the "bridegroom" (Christ) and His "bride" (the Church) takes place (Revelation 19:7-8) followed by "the marriage supper of the Lamb" (Revelation 19:9).

John 14:1-3: *"Do not let your hearts be troubled. Trust in God; trust also in me. In my father's house there are many rooms; if it were not so, I would have told you so. I am going back to prepare a place for you. And if I go and prepare a place for you, I will come back and take you to be with me so that you may also be where I am."* This passage confirms the idea of the bridegroom returning to his "Father's house" (see also John 14:28), "to prepare a place (for his followers)". Then in verse 3 we see that Christ will come back to take His followers with Him (a Rapture reference) to the Father's house in order to be with Him. This is clearly a very different description than the detailed description of the "glorious appearing" (Second Coming) which occurs at the end of the Tribulation and is described in detail in Revelation 19. The Second Coming scriptures describe

Jesus as coming to earth "with his saints" to set up his kingdom, and contain no description of being "taken" with Christ to the dwelling place He has prepared for us. In the Second Coming, Jesus comes *with* His saints, who are already in heaven, not *for* His saints as stated in John 14:1-3.

A Mystery is Revealed!

1 Corinthians 15:39-50 gives the Church entirely new information, as the introduction by Paul describes a "mystery". Starting with verse 39, Paul introduces the topic which describes the differences in "earthly bodies" and "heavenly bodies" as being distinctly different. 1 Corinthians 15:39-50 describe the following:

"All flesh is not the same...There are also heavenly bodies and there are earthly bodies; but the splendor of the heavenly bodies is one kind, and the splendor of the earthly bodies is another....So it will be with the resurrection of the dead. The body that is sown is perishable, it is raised imperishable; it is sown in dishonor, it is raised in glory; it is sown in weakness, it is raised in power; it is sown a natural body, it is raised a spiritual body....I declare to you, brothers, that flesh and blood cannot inherit the kingdom of God, nor does the perishable inherit the imperishable."

In other words, our present body of flesh and blood, which must be sustained by elements of the earth (which are perishable), must be changed to another form – a new form which is suited for the spiritual, imperishable, eternal atmosphere of heaven. This scripture makes the obvious point that we cannot enter Heaven in our current, earthly bodies which are "perishable". Additionally, we can understand from this verse that the "dead" will be resurrected with a new "heavenly" body, often referred to as a "glorified body". As pointed out by Hal Lindsey in "The Rapture" (2), the resurrected Lord Jesus reveals certain details about this resurrected body: He could appear and disappear at will (Luke 24:31 and John 20:19), thus having the ability to transcend time and space. He could move through solid walls (John 20:19), He could be seen and felt (Matthew 28:9 and Luke 24:36-42), He could eat food, although it apparently wasn't necessary (Luke 24:41-43), and He could be recognized although He was in his glorified body (Luke 24:30-31). Our resurrected bodies will no longer experience death, aging, crying, morning, sorrow or pain (Revelation 21:4).

1 Corinthians 15:51-54 confirms this unveiling of a mystery: *"Listen, I tell you a mystery: We will not all sleep, but we will all be changed – in a flash, in a twinkling of an eye, at the last trumpet. For the trumpet will sound, the dead will be raised imperishable and we will be changed. For the perishable must clothe itself with the imperishable and the mortal with immortality. When the perishable has been clothed with the imperishable, and the mortal with the immortality, then the saying that is written will come true: 'Death has been swallowed up in victory.'"*

First, Paul introduces a "mystery", which signals that he is about to reveal a new truth, previously unknown to believers. Because the Second Coming of Christ was not a mystery in the Old Testament, Paul is also signaling that he is not discussing the Second Coming. The use of this word is like a red flag, signaling that something completely new is about to be revealed. The word in the original Greek is "mysterion" which, as used in the New Testament means something previously not known, but now revealed to the believer. This new concept reveals that not all Christians will face death – that there will come a future time in which believers will "in a flash", "in the twinkling of an eye", will instantly experience a profound bodily transformation. The Greek word "allasso" means "be changed" or "to be transformed".

At this precise moment, all Christians will be transformed in body and nature into new bodies which are suited for the eternal, spiritual, incorruptible realm of Heaven, or "the Father's house". This event is clearly and significantly different from those events described at the time of the Second Coming in Revelation 19, where no such change is described. This scripture from 1 Corinthians refutes the commonly held notion that only "souls" will spend eternity in Heaven. A literal interpretation dictates that we will have an actual body; a resurrected, glorified body similar to, if not identical to the resurrected body of Jesus.

The fact that Paul stated "We **all** will be changed" indicates that the entire Church will experience this event. We also read that *"the dead will be raised imperishable"*, thus representing a description of the dead believers being raised and given their "resurrected" or "incorruptible" bodies. This specific event will take place immediately prior to the Rapture of the living believers.

To summarize the information given in 1 Corinthians we see the following:

- The Rapture was unknown until it was revealed to the Church by Paul.
- All believers living when this event (Rapture) occurs will not experience physical death.
- The Rapture will occur suddenly, without specific warning, and will be instantaneous.
- First, the dead believers will be raised and receive their incorruptible, "glorified" bodies, followed by the living believers, who will be instantly transformed from mortal to immortal ("glorified" bodies).

Letters of Clarification

Thessalonians: Perhaps more than any other book in the Bible, the context of these letters is of great importance. In both letters (1 and 2 Thessalonians) it is clear that Paul is following up on previous discussions, and understanding the context of these discussions is helpful in understanding the scriptures. As we see in 2 Thessalonians 2:5, *"Do you not remember that while I was still with you, I was telling you these things?"*

1 Thessalonians: The context behind these passages includes the fact that Paul is giving certain assurances to believers concerning those who die before Christ returns. Their questions apparently related to the fact that since Paul's visit to Thessalonica, some believers had died (have fallen "asleep"), and these followers were curious as to the fate of their deceased loved ones upon the Lords' return. In the first letter to the Thessalonians, Paul answered the questions of whether believers who have died will be reunited with those believers who are still living at the time of the Rapture.

1 Thessalonians 4:13: *"Brothers, we do not want you to be ignorant about those who fall asleep or to grieve like the rest of men, who have no hope. We believe that Jesus died and rose again and so we believe that God will bring with Jesus those who have fallen asleep in him."*

1 Thessalonians 4:16-18: *"For the Lord himself will come down from heaven with a loud command, and with the voice of an archangel and with the trumpet call of God, and **the dead in Christ will rise first. After that, we who are still alive and are left will be caught up together with them in the clouds to meet the Lord in the air.** And so we will be with the Lord forever. Therefore encourage each other with these words."*

Just like the scriptures in 1 Corinthians, Paul describes the scenario of the *"dead, in Christ"* rising first and then, those who are alive at that time will *"meet the Lord in the air"*. Importantly, we see that unlike the Second Coming scriptures (Rev. 19), where Christ physically comes to earth, in this instance Christ meets his believers *"in the air"*.

Several specific events occur: 1) The Lord will *"come down from heaven with a shout"*, which is the shout of resurrection. *"The voice of an archangel"* is thought to signal that Michael is to lead Israel for the seven year tribulation, as he did in the Old Testament, 2) The dead believers will rise first, 3) *"Then we which are still alive and remain shall be **caught up** together with them in the clouds..."* The phrase "caught up" is taken from the Greek word **"harpazo"** meaning **"to snatch up"** suddenly and without warning. This clarification of these events, as given by Paul is meant to give encouragement and comfort to these believers.

Paul continues with his reasoning and gives further details in 1 Thessalonians 5:

1 Thessalonians 5:2-3: *"for you know very well that **the day of the Lord** will come like a thief in the night. **While people are saying 'peace and safety', destruction will come on them suddenly**, as labor pains on a pregnant woman, and they will not escape. But you, brethren, are not in darkness, that the day should overtake you like a thief; for you are all sons of light and sons of day..."*

1 Thessalonians 5:9-11: *"For **God did not appoint us to suffer wrath** but to receive salvation through our Lord Jesus Christ... Therefore encourage one another and build each other up, just as you are doing."*

"The Day of the Lord", is a term which is used multiple times in the Old Testament and is used to refer to a time of God's judgment on the world. In addition, the terms "the last days" or "in that day" which are similar terms, are seen multiple times in the Old Testament. Among the references in the Old Testament are Isaiah 2:12-21, 13, 9-16, 34:1-8, Joel 1:15, 2:1-11, 2:28-32, 3:9-12, Amos, 5: 18-20 and Zephaniah 1:7-18. Research of Old Testament prophecies reveal that the term the *"Day of the Lord"* is a time of God's judgment, cumulating in the Second Coming of Christ, and followed by a time of special divine blessing to be fulfilled in the millennial kingdom.

"Peace and safety" indicates that the nation of Israel will be calling for "peace and safety". This represents the situation which is both desired in today's world and it also represents the coming peace and safety which the Antichrist will confirm with his "peace" covenant. However this apparent peace and safety will be short-lived as the Antichrist will break the covenant at the mid-point of the Tribulation and begin the period of intense persecution of believers worldwide, *"...destruction will come on them suddenly"*. Once this period begins, there will be increasing frequency and severity of the *"labor pains on a pregnant woman"*, a description of how the various judgments will unfold during the Tribulation.

The destruction which occurs "suddenly" will only affect those who are "living in darkness." However, unlike those living in darkness (unsaved) the Church, will not experience the Tribulation because of their salvation.

"But you brethren are not in darkness, that the day should overtake you like a thief." Paul now describes that "the day of the Lord" will not take believers by surprise for two main reasons, 1) because the believer is a child of "light" and the "day", meaning that the believer, filled with the Holy Spirit and the scriptures of prophecy should

possess the knowledge to which Paul is referring. These believers will know the general time leading to the Tribulation because of their understanding of the prophecies, and 2) because the believer is not destined for the wrath (Tribulation), *"For God has not destined us for wrath..."*, the Church will experience the Rapture prior to the beginning of the Tribulation. To summarize 1 Thessalonians we gain the following information:

- The idea of the Rapture was taught to believers in Thessalonica.
- Believers will not be "overtaken" by the Tribulation. To not be "overtaken" assumes that you will not come in contact with nor experience in any way - the Tribulation.
- The Rapture will deliver believers from the "wrath", also known as the "Day of the Lord". This is based upon salvation, thus only believers will experience the Rapture.
- All living believers will be suddenly caught up to meet the Lord in the air; at which time they will be reunited with loved ones who have died in Christ.
- The Day of the Lord or the Tribulation will come with sudden destruction upon the unsuspecting, non-believing world, at a time when "peace and safety" is being proclaimed. The Rapture will have delivered the body of believers (The Church) from this scenario.
- Knowledge of the Rapture as occurring prior to the wrath (Tribulation) should be a source of comfort and encouragement to the believer.

2 Thessalonians: The context given in this book tells us that confusion existed among the believers in Thessalonica regarding *"The day of the Lord"*, as many believers thought that this period was already in progress. They were experiencing persecution and hardships and thus reasoned that they were actually enduring the Tribulation. Also, someone had apparently brought them a message, falsely representing Paul, which said that the day of the Lord had already begun. Paul clarifies matters in the 2 Thessalonians 2: 1-2:

> *"Concerning the coming of our Lord Jesus Christ and our being gathered to him, we ask you, brothers, not to become easily alarmed by some prophecy, letter or report supposed to have come from us, saying that the day of the Lord has already come.* **Let no man deceive you by any means: for that day shall not come, except there come a falling away first, and that man of sin be revealed,** *the son of perdition."(KJV)*

The phrase *"...our being gathered to him"* references the Rapture, as a gathering together of the Church as described in 1 Thessalonians 4:15-17.

Paul is revealing that they should not be "alarmed", because that day of the Lord has not yet come. He tells them that first, before that day, two specific events would occur: 1) *"for that day will not come, except there come a falling away first."*, and 2) *"and that man of sin be revealed, the son of perdition."* The Greek word "apostesia" means "departure" or "falling away". Many translate this to mean a falling away from faith, or what is also called apostasy (1). However, there are several reasons this reference to the "departure" could actually represent the Rapture rather than a "falling away" in faith. In this context, Paul is giving a specific event, which could be referenced by the believers indicating that the Tribulation had begun. During the time of his letter to the Thessalonians, there were already false teachings and apostasy, as evidenced by the forged letter. Referencing apostasy as a specific event that needed to occur before the Antichrist is revealed would not be reassuring to this church, nor would it be specifically identifiable for the same reason. Therefore it is quite possible that the "falling away" more accurately describes "departure" as the departure of the Church at the time of the Rapture.

Additionally, to bolster the concept that this verse is describing the Rapture, the Rapture would have been a specific, identifiable event for the Thessalonians. Recall from the context that Paul was attempting to give reassurance that this Church was **not** living in the midst of the Tribulation and Paul was giving "hope" and "encouragement" to the Thessalonians. Also of importance in understanding this scripture is the fact that the early translations of the Bible (preceding the KJV) used the word "departure" to describe this event, rather than "falling away." The verses in 2 Thessalonians 2: 7-8 contains an identical sequence of events which plainly tell us that the Church will be removed before the unveiling of the Antichrist. Using the term "departure" in a literal sense would perfectly parallel this similar and related scripture found in 2 Thessalonians 2:7-8. However, if the true meaning of this word is "apostasy" or a falling away in faith, then the message would be very similar; Paul would, in this interpretation, still be stating that the Thessalonians are not living in the "Day of the Lord", and that a "departure from faith", or apostasy in the Church.

Both interpretations, either "departure" as a reference to the Rapture or understanding "departure" to mean "departure from faith" are both consistent with all other writings of end time events. There is ample evidence to suggest that apostasy will be taking place at the end of the age, making this view consistent with other related scriptures. There also seem to be plenty of evidence that the scripture is pointing to the Rapture, in which case the interpretation would give great consistency with 2 Thessalonians 2:6-8 (below).

> **2 Thessalonians 2:6-9**: *"And now you know what restrains him (Antichrist) now, so that in his time he may be revealed. For the mystery of lawlessness is already at work;* ***only he who now restrains will keep on doing so until he is taken out of the way. And then the lawless one will be revealed*** *whom the Lord Jesus will overthrow with the breath of his mouth and destroy with the splendor of his coming. The coming of the lawless one will be in accordance with the work of Satan, displayed in all kinds of counterfeit miracles, signs and wonders."*

Here, the "restrainer" clearly refers to the Holy Spirit's presence in the Church, as this interpretation represents the best answer to the grammatical, contextual and theological questions in 2 Thessalonians. Other possibilities as to the identification of the restrainer, such as human government or some powerful human figure seem highly unlikely. Understanding the role of the restrainer further confirms that it must be the Holy Spirit residing within the Church: *first,* this restraint must represent a worldwide influence which suggests omnipresence; *second,* the restrainer must have supernatural power in order to be able restrain such potent forces such as worldwide apostasy and the emergence of the Antichrist; *third,* the restrainer must have some logical reason for ending the restraint of lawlessness and the ability of the Antichrist to seize absolute power. There is simply no other likely choice than the Church, including the presence of the Holy Spirit as representing this Restrainer (2, 3). In addition, the scripture speaks of the Holy Spirit as the One who restrains evil (4), both in the world (Genesis 6:3) and in the heart of the believer (Galatians 5:16-17).

This "restraint" most likely includes both a spiritual and literal restraint. Spiritually, the presence of the Holy Spirit on earth has a restraining influence upon evil. Man alone or any form of government is unable to do this. All things which occur during the Tribulation seem to confirm this view – that the Tribulation becomes the hour of darkness with false apostles and ministers working within a completely false religion. All of God's word will be neglected and the Antichrist will be embraced, with the world under his reign. Literally, if the Church was present at the unveiling of the Antichrist, then many believers would know and recognize the Antichrist for who he is. This would severely restrict his ability to gain power: if there was ongoing debate regarding his identity as the Antichrist, then it would be difficult at best for him to gain any level of prominence or unilateral support. However, once the "restrainer" is removed – he will be revealed, and can assume his power unencumbered by the presence of the Church. This was the assurance Paul was giving the Thessalonians – that they couldn't be living during the Tribulation, because the Church must be removed first. Note the chronology of events: 1) the restrainer is removed, 2) the lawless one (Antichrist) is revealed, and 3) Jesus will destroy him and then begin His 1,000 reign on earth. After the restrainer is removed, we see what the Antichrist will be able to accomplish without the restraining influence of the Church, in 2 Thessalonians 2:9-12:

"The coming of the lawless one will be in accordance with the work of Satan displayed

*in all kinds of counterfeit miracles, signs and
wonders, and in every sort of evil that
deceives those who are perishing. They
perish because they refused to love the truth
and so be saved. For this reason God sends
them a powerful delusion so that they will
believe the lie and so that all will be
condemned who have not believed the truth
but have delighted in wickedness."*

After the restrainer is removed, the Antichrist, in accordance with Satan, will be allowed to counterfeit many of the previous miracles of Jesus. This will help him deceive the world into following him. At this time, the unbelieving world will be opened to "every sort of evil". In addition, God sends them a powerful delusion so that they believe the lie, which is most likely the Antichrist's claim to be God.

In summary, 2 Thessalonians reveals the following:

- The "day of the Lord" (Tribulation) had not yet started during Paul's writing to the Thessalonians, despite their fears of such.
- The Church with the Holy Spirit must be removed before the Antichrist can be revealed. This represents the removal of the Church at the time of the Rapture.
- Once the Church and the Holy Spirit are removed, the Antichrist will be revealed.
- The coming of the Antichrist will be in accordance with (in harmony with) Satan, and will be displayed by many counterfeit miracles, signs and wonders, and every sort of evil (see also Matt. 24:24).
- God will send a powerful delusion so that

they (the non-believers) will believe a lie. They will also be condemned because they have not believed the truth and because they have "delighted in wickedness."

Revelation and the Rapture

There are additional scriptural references contained within the book of Revelation that provide significant information regarding the Rapture. The first three chapters of Revelation consist of the letters to the seven churches. It appears that all letters were to be sent to all churches. We see in Revelation 1: 11 *"Write on a scroll what you see and send it to the seven churches..."* and each letter contained the verse, *"He who has an ear, let him hear what the spirit says to the churches."* Note the plural nature "churches" rather than directing each individual letter only to that specific church. All Christians are intended to gain information from all of these letters to these churches.

Revelation 3:10: This scripture, which comes from the letter to the church of Philadelphia, contains key information. The context of this letter indicates that it pertains to the Church (the body of believers) existing at the time just preceding the Rapture, Tribulation and Second Coming, as seen in Revelation 3:10-11: *"Since you have kept my command to endure patiently,* **I will also keep you from the hour of trial that is going to come upon the whole world to test those who live on the earth. I am coming soon.** *Hold on to what you have, so that no one will take your crown."* This scripture is a specific message to "the Church" in existence during the time just before the "coming soon" of Christ (for the reference of the "crown", see 2 Timothy 4:8 and 2 Peter 5:4). The phrase, *"Those who dwell on earth", or "the whole world",* contains a clear reference to the people living on earth during the tribulation period, and represents (initially) non-believers. This is one of four specific scriptural references that the Church will not undergo the Tribulation. The other references are 1 Thessalonians 1:10, 1Thessalonians 5:9, and 2 Peter 2:5-9.

Also noteworthy is the fact that the scripture states: *"I will keep you from **the hour of trial**"*. This point is significant because some scholars believe that Christians will experience the Tribulation, but will somehow be protected while living through this seven year period. That thought however is inconsistent with the scriptures which clearly state that believers will be kept **from** "the hour", or "the time" of the trial. This serves to indicate that the Church will not be present for that entire period of **time**, not just protected from the **events** themselves.

Further analysis of this letter gives us even more pertinent information. Revelation 3:12 states the following: *"Him who overcomes I will make a pillar in the temple of my God. Never again will he leave it. I will write on him the name of my God and the name of my city of my God, the new Jerusalem, which is coming down out of heaven from my God..."* Jesus now introduces the subject of *"**new Jerusalem, which is coming down out of heaven...**"* I believe that this scripture represents the dwelling place of the raptured believers during the Tribulation and beyond. The evidence for this is found later in Revelation. After the 1,000 year millennial reign of Christ, we can see in **Revelation 21:2, *"I saw the Holy City, the new Jerusalem, coming down out of heaven from God, prepared as a bride beautifully dressed for her husband"*** and **Revelation 21:9-10, *"Come, I will show you the bride, the wife of the Lamb. And he carried me away in the spirit...and showed me the Holy City, Jerusalem, coming down out of heaven from God."*** This seems to serve as a representation of where the Church resides during both the Tribulation period and during the 1,000 reign of Christ. By saying *"I will show you the bride, the wife of the Lamb"* immediately followed by describing New Jerusalem, *"and showed me the Holy City, Jerusalem, coming down out of heaven from God."* This scripture clarifies where the Church has been residing – in New Jerusalem.

Revelation 19:7 gives a description of heaven, as it appears immediately before the Second Coming when John sees a vision of the Church engaging in worship: *"Let us rejoice and be glad and give him glory. **For the wedding of the Lamb has come, and his bride has made herself ready. Fine linen, bright and clean, was given her to wear (fine linen stands for the righteous acts of the saints).**"* The wedding has already occurred and it took place in heaven sometime prior to the Second Coming. Because this wedding took place before the Second Coming, it creates a strong argument that the Church, following the Rapture, has been in heaven in order for the wedding to take place. Additionally, we see a clear reference of the Church, who has been purified through the blood of Jesus for the Bema judgment: *"the bride has made herself ready. Fine linen, bright and clean was given her to wear"*. A few scriptures later we see Christ in His appearance at the Second Coming, in Rev. 19:11 and 19:14:

> *"I saw heaven standing open and there before me was a white horse, whose rider is called Faithful and True. With justice he judges and makes war...The armies of heaven were following him, riding on white horses and **dressed in fine linen, white and clean.**"*

This description represents the Church which the scripture tells us, is coming to earth with Jesus. Revelation 19:7 explained who was *"dressed in fine linen, white and clean"* as being *"the bride"* which is another name for the Church. Thus, taking the scripture literally, if the Church has been in heaven during the Tribulation, and is now coming to earth with Christ at the Second Coming, then the only conclusion is that the Church had been raptured prior to the Tribulation. This is completely consistent with the four specific scriptures which state that the Church will be saved from the "hour of trial".

The book of Revelation gives us additional information regarding the Rapture. In the first chapter of Revelation, just as John initially experienced Jesus in his presence (after hearing "a loud voice, like a trumpet"), we read Revelation 1:12: *"I turned around to see the voice that was speaking to me. And when I turned I saw seven golden lampstands (candlesticks) and among the lampstands was someone like a son of man...In his right hand he held seven stars, and out of his mouth came a sharp double-edged sword."* The meaning of the lampstands is explained later in Revelation 1:20, *"The seven stars are the angels of the seven churches, and the seven lampstands are the seven churches."*

This scripture clarifies that the seven lampstands represent the Church. There is a significant parallel between this explanation and scripture in **Revelation 4.** Revelation 4 begins with John's ascension to Heaven which takes place just prior to the Tribulation. As John initially takes in the view of Heaven, he sees the following, as described in Revelation 4:5, **"Before the throne, seven lamps were blazing. These are the seven spirits of God."** The fact that the seven lampstands have just been identified as the Church strongly suggests that these same lampstands (the Church) are now in Heaven, and are now burning. This may represent that the Church, like John, has now ascended to Heaven following the Rapture. Here, they are called the spirits of God, because John is emphasizing that the Holy Spirit indwells all believers of all churches (i.e., the seven churches representing all churches is clear from Revelation 1-3). Granted, there are other representations in the Bible which reference burning lamps and candles, and the number seven, however **the most recent description is that given in Revelation 1:20,** which defines the meaning as the Church. That fact seems compelling for our understanding of interpreting these seven lamps –the fact that Revelation gave us the explanation only a few chapters earlier.

Further study of the book of Revelation gives us important additional information. The first three chapters deal exclusively with the Church and the Church is mentioned 19 times in these first three chapters. Following this, in Chapters 4-18, which contains very detailed information about the Tribulation period, there is **no mention of the Church.** The next mention of the Church is found at the time of the Second Coming as written in Revelation 19:7. This obvious omission is another indication that the Church is not present on earth during the Tribulation.

Yet another reference to the Rapture as described in the book of Revelation, can be found in the actual sequence of events given. In the first chapter of Revelation, we see that Jesus is speaking to John: Revelation 1:19 *"Write, therefore, what you have seen, what is now, and what must take place later."* The KJV reads as follows, *"Write the things which thou hast seen, and the things which are and the things which shall be hereafter."*

First, John is told to write about *"what you have seen".* John had just seen Jesus – in Chapter 1, the first thing that John saw was the very presence of Jesus. Thus, the term *"what you have seen"* serves as a reference to the fact that John had just seen Jesus. The description given was in the past tense, thus describing something John had seen.

The next phrase *"and the things which are"*, or *"what is now"*, describes Chapters 2 and 3, or the Church Age.

These chapters are described in the present tense, and was ongoing (i.e., the "Church Age") during John's life. The Church Age on earth will last until the time of the Rapture, thus, *"the things which are"*, represents the "things" ongoing at the time of John's life.

The next phrase, *"and what must take place later"* is a clear reference to the future, or what must take place following these first two phrases given in the verse. This will consist of the description of the Tribulation which is described next in the chronology of Revelation, or Revelation 4-19.

Chapter 4 of Revelation occurs just after the conclusion of this full description of the Church Age seen in chapters 1-3. We see in Revelation 4:1 the following: *"After this, I looked, and there before me was a door standing open in heaven. And the voice I had first heard speaking to me like a trumpet said, 'Come up here, and I will show you what must take place after this.'"* The term *"after this"* is used twice in this verse. Because Jesus had just completed discussions of the Church Age (chapters 1-3), it is logical to assume that *"after this"* or *"after these things"*, means **after the Church Age has concluded.** This idea is bolstered by the fact that the Church is not mentioned again in the book of Revelation until the appearance with Jesus at the Second Coming. Following the second use of *"after this"*, the book of Revelation begins the detailed description of the seven year Tribulation.

In summary, the sequence of these events can be seen chronologically: 1) Jesus appeared to John ("what you have seen"), 2) The Church Age is discussed in Chapters 1-3 ("the things which are"), 3) John ascends to heaven, and 4) John sees all of the events of the tribulation period ("what must take place later"). Similarly, in Revelation, Chapter 19, which is a description of events just after the Tribulation, also begins with the phrase "After this", which, in this case clearly refers to the period "after" the Tribulation. The sending of John's spirit to heaven is seen as a representation of the Church being raptured. The parallels between Revelation 4:1 and 1 Thessalonians 4:16-17 are interesting and compelling. Both passages describe a sequence of events which describe the sound of a trumpet sounding and the shout of a command, then followed by the act of being caught up to heaven.

Saved from the Wrath

There are four specific references that the Church will be spared from the Tribulation, thus indicating that the Rapture will take place before this seven year period.

- 2 Peter 2:5-9: *"...he did not spare the ancient world when he brought the flood on its ungodly people, **but protected Noah, a preacher of righteousness, and seven others;** if he condemned the cities of Sodom and Gomorrah by burning them to ashes, and made them an example of what is going to happen to the ungodly; **and if he rescued Lot, a righteous man,** who was distressed by the filthy lives of lawless men...**if this is so, then the Lord knows how to rescue godly men from trials and to hold the unrighteous for the day of judgment...**"* The information contained here is very pertinent. First, Peter is saying that there are past examples of godly men being saved from God's judgments or "trials". This dispels the feeling among some believers that there is no basis that Christians should be saved from the Tribulation. Secondly, it confirms that God has made direct judgments upon earth in the past. Peter reminds us of this fact and confirms that both the flood and the destruction of Sodom and Gomorrah were real events which actually occurred as written. Peter then gives examples of those instances in which God's wrath has involved believers being spared. He reminds us that God saved Noah from the flood and God also spared Lot's life just prior to the destruction of Sodom and Gomorrah. The events which occurred in Egypt (Passover) during the time of Moses are yet additional examples of Godly men being spared from God's judgment. Thus, the issue of God sparing believers from his judgment is a recurrent theme in the Bible.

- 1 Thessalonians 1:10: *"and to wait for his Son from heaven, whom he raised from the dead – Jesus, who rescues us from the coming wrath"*

- 1 Thessalonians 5:9: *"For God did not appoint us to suffer wrath but to receive salvation through our Lord Jesus Christ."*

- Revelation 3:10: *"Since you have kept my command to endure patiently, I will also keep you from the hour of trial that is going to come upon the whole world..."*

From these scriptures we have important information conveyed to the Church. A literal interpretation of these scriptures indicates that the Church will not endure the Tribulation. This is also fitting with the imagery of the Church as the bride of Christ. It seems unthinkable that the bride of Christ would be forced to endure the Tribulation just before the wedding. Additionally, there are **no** Bible references which give guidance to the Church for enduring the Tribulation. The only scriptural references pertinent to the Tribulation which are directed to the Church, involve these four passages – all of which describe being saved from this period of time.

Perhaps the most important point in terms of Rapture of the Church as being an identifiable and specific event has to do with the distinct differences between the Rapture and the Second Coming. Clearly, from reading all of these pertinent scriptures, we know that the descriptions are of events occurring at the "end of the age". Thus, these events have to be describing either one single event, or two separate events. By reading the scriptures literally, it is impossible to see all of these passages as describing a single event – there are far too many inconsistencies and contradictions. However, all of these scriptures can be easily placed into two separate categories, the Rapture and the Second Coming:

10 Distinct Differences Between the Rapture and the Second Coming

Rapture:

1. Christ comes **for His own** (the Church): John 14:1-3; 1 Thessalonians 4:16-17.
2. Christ comes **in the air**: 1 Thessalonians 4:17.
3. Christ comes to **claim His bride**: 1 Thessalonians 4:16-17.
4. The Church is **taken to heaven,** with Christ: John 14:1-3; Revelation 4:5, 19:7-8.
5. The Rapture can occur at **any time**: Matthew: 24:36-42; Mark 13:32.
6. The Rapture will happen **instantly**: 1 Corinthians 15:52.
7. The Antichrist begins his **world rule**: 2 Thessalonians 2:6-12; Revelation 13:7-8.
8. The **Tribulation begins**: 2 Thessalonians 2:6-12.
9. Only **believers** will see Christ: 1 Thessalonians 4:16-17.

10. Christ comes **for the Church**: 1 Thessalonians 4:14-17; 1 Corinthians 15:50-58.

Second Coming:

1. Christ comes **with His own** (the Church): Revelation 19:14.
2. Christ comes **to the earth**: Zechariah 14:4-5; Acts 1:11.
3. Christ comes **with His bride**: Revelation 19:6-14.
4. Christ sets up His kingdom **on earth**: Revelation 20.
5. Occurs at the **end of the Tribulation**: Daniel 9:24-27; Matthew 24: 29.
6. Occurs with a specific **sequence of events**: Revelation 19; Zechariah 14:3-5; Matthew 24: 29-31.
7. The Antichrist will be **destroyed**: Revelation 19:20.
8. The **millennial reign** begins: Revelation 20:1-7.
9. **Every eye** will see Christ: Matthew 24:30; Revelation 1:7.
10. **For** redeemed **Israel and Gentiles**: Romans 11:25-27; Matthew 25:31-46.

By reviewing these scriptures in the context of two separate events, it is easy to see how the first event to occur is the Rapture, and then followed by the second "event"; the Second Coming of Christ. It is impossible to take all of these scriptures and combine them into a single event without numerous glaring inconsistencies. To combine these events into one scenario requires extensive allegories and symbolism of the scripture. In contrast, a literal interpretation of the same scriptures confirms the reality of the occurrence of two separate events (the Rapture and the Second Coming). Once the scriptures are read in this literal context, then the two discreet and different events can be seen. Such a literal interpretation requires no "explaining away" through neither allegory nor twisting the words to fit into a doctrine; rather, with a literal understanding, the scriptures can stand alone without the requirement of additional "explanations".

To summarize, we have seen that the most literal understanding of scripture give us ample evidence for the Rapture of the Church occurring as a singular event which precedes the Tribulation. This is commonly referred to as the "Pre-Tribulation Rapture". The imagery of the Church as the bride of Christ, and the wedding customs of 2,000 years ago serve as a perfect example describing the events of the Rapture. We also have compelling evidence from the scriptures that the Church is not expected to endure the Tribulation. There is no scripture informing the Church that it would experience the Tribulation, nor does the Bible contain any warning or advice for the Church in terms of how to live through the Tribulation.

In contrast however, Paul gave extensive information regarding the Rapture of the Church; information which is distinctly different from the detailed scriptures describing the Second Coming of Christ. The description of John ascending to heaven in Revelation 4:1 is identical to the description of the Rapture of the Church given by Paul in 1 Thessalonians 4:16. The obvious omission of any mention of the Church in Revelation 4-19, where the Tribulation is described in a detailed manner, bolsters the idea that the Church is residing in heaven after the Rapture. To add to this idea, we finally see the Church returning from heaven with Christ at the Second Coming. A literal understanding of these scriptures makes perfect sense and requires no "allegory" or "twisting" of the scriptures. Further, by understanding the Rapture as a pre-tribulation event (thus the term "Pre-Tribulation Rapture) gives full consistency with the message of "hope" and "comfort" that is conveyed in the context of these end time scriptures.

CHAPTER NINE NOTES

1. Charles Ryrie. What You Should Know About the Rapture (Moody Press. 1981).
2. Hal Lindsey. The Rapture (Bantam Books. 1984).
3. John F. Walvoord. The Rapture Question (Zondervan Publishing House. 1979).
4. Mark Hitchcock and Thomas Ice. The Truth Behind Left Behind (Multnomah Publishers, Inc. 2004).

TEN

REVELATION: THE CHURCH, THE TRIBULATION AND BEYOND

Revelation 1:3: Blessed is the one who reads the words of this prophecy, and blessed are those who hear it and take to heart what is written in it, because the time is near.

Revelation 22:7: Behold, I am coming soon! Blessed is he who keeps the words of the prophecy in this book.

The Letters to the Churches

The Seven Churches: The first three chapters of Revelation are focused on a series of letters which were sent to the seven churches located in the region of Asia. There were more than seven churches in that region, but only seven were chosen to receive messages. These letters give the Church important information and guidance on how we should/should not live as part of the body of the Church. These seven letters indicate a representation of the types of churches that will exist throughout church history. Jesus specifically told John to write the information which He provided, on a scroll and then to send it to the seven churches. Revelation 1:11, *"Write on a scroll what you see and send it to the seven churches: to Ephesus, Smyrna,*

Pergamum, Thyatira, Sardis, Philadelphia and Laodicea."
Each of the letters follows a specific format (1):

- **Destination:** The city where the church is located and historical background.
- **Description of Christ:** in each letter Christ gives a description of himself which meets an existing need in that church.
- **Commendation:** Christ praises each church for something, but for the churches of Thyatira (counterfeit church) and Laodicea (apostate church).
- **Rebuke:** the only churches Christ doesn't rebuke are Smyrna (suffering church) and Philadelphia (missionary church).
- **Exhortation:** Christ counsels and encourages each of His churches to add what is needed to make them more Godly and to remove anything that hinders their relationship with Christ.
- **Promise:** Christ promises blessings to all who "has an ear" and heeds Christ's advice to the church and the individuals in it.
- **Prophetic Application:** This is the historical rule which each church was to play during the subsequent centuries.

In summary, the letters to the seven churches give important lessons of how to live our lives as believers in Christ, living and serving as members of the Church. Perhaps the most succinct and pertinent review has been written by John Walvoord which is paraphrased below (2):

- **Ephesus:** represents *the danger of losing our first love,* that intense love and devotion to Christ which is often seen early in the "relationship", but can later decrease in intensity over time.

- **Smyrna:** represents *the danger of fear of suffering.* They were advised by Christ to "fear none of these things that they would suffer." In this day, when the persecution of the saints has been revived, this is a message of perseverance; "Be faithful to death and I will give you the Crown of Life."
- **Pergamos:** represents *the danger of doctrinal compromise.* This message is consistent with the themes in Matthew 24/25 and 2 Peter. False teachings/false teachers are repetitively warned against, particularly in the context of the time during the end of the church age
- **Thyatira:** represents *the danger of moral compromise.* The church today often tolerates and/or encourages a compromise of the moral standards described in the Bible.
- **Sardis:** represents a warning against *the danger of spiritual deadness.* Here, Christ reveals that the outward appearance or the reputation was that of an "alive" church, but in reality, they were "dead". This is similar to what Christ said to the Pharisees, "Outside they looked like lovely, newly white-washed tombs, but on the inside they were full of dead men's bones"
- **Philadelphia:** represents *to keep enduring with patience.* There was no rebuke for this church. Jesus praised this church for their "work" which was obviously evangelism.

- **Laodicea:** represents a warning against *the danger of being lukewarm* in matters of love and devotion to Christ, and being unaware of their spiritual needs because they were *"rich and increased with goods and have need of nothing..."*

Special Messages in Revelation

- **Revelation 1:3:** *"Blessed is the one who reads the words of this prophecy, and blessed are those who hear it and take to heart what is written in it, because the time is near."*

- **Revelation 22:7:** *"Behold, I am coming soon! Blessed is he who keeps the words of the prophecy in this book"*

- **Revelation 22:20:** *"He who testifies to these things says, Yes, I am coming soon."* From the above scriptures in Revelation, it seems to indicate that once we have an *understanding* of the words; Jesus will be *"coming soon."* To "testify" one must have understanding. In order to *"keep the words"* of the book, one must also have an understanding. To *"take to heart"* also implies that understanding must take place first. The common theme from these scriptures, from both Daniel and Revelation indicates that once an understanding of both books takes place, then the time is very near for the return of Christ. Interestingly, not until the end of the twentieth century did the world see an explosion of books and literature describing the book in a literal way. This alone gives compelling evidence that we are living in the latter days.

- **Revelation 22:18:** *"I warn everyone who hears the*

words of this book: If anyone adds anything to them, God will add to him the plagues described in this book. And if anyone takes words away from this book of prophecy, God will take away from him his share in the tree of life and in the holy city, which are described in this book."

The 21 Judgments of the Tribulation

• **Revelation 6:1-2:** *"I watched as the lamb opened the* **first of the seven seals.** *Then I heard one of the four living creatures say in a voice like thunder, 'Come!' I looked and there before me was a* **white horse!** *Its rider held a bow, and he was given a crown, and he rode out as a conqueror bent on conquest."* Because Christ has opened this seal, "allowing" the rider on the white horse to be released, and because this first seal initiates the following judgments – this rider is felt to be the Antichrist. In addition, this marks the beginning of the Tribulation, and we know from Daniel 9:27 that the Antichrist gains power at the beginning of the seven year Tribulation. In addition, the Antichrist will appear on the world scene at the beginning of the Tribulation, just as described here. This rider holds a bow without an arrow, thus indicating that he, the Antichrist will "conquer" via peace, initially. The bow also indicates that this individual will have control of weapons of war. The white horse, in ancient times indicates conquest; when a victor triumphantly entered a newly conquered kingdom, he would ride a white horse. Also, note that on his head rests a crown which is a crown of a victor (Greek: *stephanos*), indicating that he has indeed succeeded in his quest to "conquer" (2).

- **Revelation 6:3-4:** *"When the lamb **opened the second seal**...Then another horse came out, a fiery red one. Its rider was given power to take peace from the earth and to make men slay each other. To him was given a large sword."* Peace has now been taken from the world, and warfare begins. From subsequent descriptions in Revelation, it is apparent that warfare occupies much of the time during this last seven year period.

- **Revelation 6:5-6:** *"When the lamb **opened the third seal**, I heard the third living creature say, 'Come!' I looked, and there before me was a **black horse**! Its rider was holding a pair of scales in his hand. Then I heard what sounded like a voice among the four living creatures, saying, 'A quart of wheat for a day's wages, and three quarts of barley for a day's wages, and do not damage the oil and the wine.'"* This passage indicates that in the aftermath of this first war, subsequent famine and financial collapse will occur, and life will then be reduced to the barest of necessities – where a full day's work will only buy enough food for one day – and nothing else. This picture is bolstered by the indication of the black horse, which is the symbol of suffering (Lam. 5: 10).

- **Revelation 6:7-8:** *"When the lamb **opened the fourth seal**, I heard the voice of the fourth living creature say, 'Come!' I looked, and there was a **pale horse**! Its rider was named Death, and Hades was following close behind him. They were given power over a fourth of the earth to kill by sword, famine and plague, and by the wild beasts of the earth."* Following the first three horsemen, we can see the aftermath of war and famine, which is death. One-fourth of the world's population will perish in death from this judgment. If this judgment were to occur with a world population of 6 billion people, then approximately 1.5 billion people would die. It should be clear that these judgments are not at all trivial, and as Jesus said (Matt. 24: 21), *"For then there would be great distress, unequaled from the beginning of the world until now – and never to be equaled again."*

• **Revelation 6:9-11:** *"When he **opened the fifth seal**, I saw under the altar **the souls of those who had been slain because of the word of God** and the testimony they had maintained. They called out in a loud voice, 'How long, Sovereign Lord, holy and true, until you judge the inhabitants of the earth and avenge our blood?' Then each of them was given a white robe, and told to wait a little longer, until the number of their fellow servants and brothers who were to be killed as they had been were completed."* The scene now shifts from earth to heaven, and John sees those who have been martyred for their faith in Christ. Because they are introduced just after the fourth seal suggests that they have come from the Tribulation. This idea is bolstered by the fact that these souls ask for judgment upon those that still dwell on earth – thus it is apparent that their persecutors are still living. They are also told to wait because other events must take place first, with additional martyrs who must be added to their numbers. They are to wait until the time of Christ's return in power and glory for the summary judgment on earth. Also noteworthy is the fact that the scripture describes "souls" which are present at the altar, indicating that they have not received their resurrected bodies, as have those believers who have been Raptured and have received their "resurrected" bodies (1 Corinthians 15:50-54). This passage also indicates that the act of declaring faith in Christ will come with a heavy price; these believers will be persecuted for their faith, and subsequently put to death. This is confirmed in Chapter 7, where we see another picture of martyred believers and in Chapter 13 where death is inflicted upon those who do not worship the beast.

- **Revelation 6:12-17:** *"I watched as he **opened the sixth seal**. There was a **great earthquake**. The sun turned black like sackcloth made of goat hair, the whole moon turned blood red, and the stars in the sky fell to earth as late figs drop from a fig tree when shaken by a strong wind. The sky receded like a scroll, rolling up, and every mountain and island was removed from its place."* Could this be a description of nuclear missiles with their detonation? The fact that the "sky receded like a scroll" is a similar description to a nuclear detonation, and the "stars in the sky" falling could indicate ICBMs re-entering the earths atmosphere. Remember – John is seeing approximately 2,000 years into the future. The sun turning "black like sackcloth" and the moon turning "blood red" could indicate the effects of "nuclear winter", as described by scientists following massive nuclear exchange. These descriptions could also indicate a meteor shower with meteors hitting earth, causing similar events to occur.

- **Revelation 8:1:** *"And he **opened the seventh seal**, there was **silence in heaven** for about half an hour. And then I saw the seven angels who stand before God and to them were given seven trumpets."* With the opening of the seventh seal, the narrative is resumed from the close of chapter 6. This absolute silence in heaven indicates that something tremendous is about to happen, and is in contrast to the earlier joyous sounds seen in chapters 4 and 5.

- **Revelation 8:7:** *"The first angel sounded his trumpet, and there came **hail and fire** mixed with blood, and it was hurled down upon the earth. A third of the earth was burned up, a third of the trees were burned up, and all the green grass was burned up."* The main burden of this judgment is the destruction of vegetation on earth which is also consistent with the aftermath of regional nuclear war.

- **Revelation 8:8:** *"The second angel sounded his trumpet, and something like a **huge mountain**, all ablaze, was thrown into the sea. **A third of the sea turned into blood, a third of the living creatures in the sea died, and a third of the ships were destroyed.**"* As John witnessed these events, he saw a significant portion of the earth – approximately a third of the sea; including sea-life and sea vessels are destroyed. Perhaps this meets the description of a huge volcano blasting the side of a mountain (recall Mount St. Helens) or a large meteor crashing into earth. The third of the sea turning to blood could be a description of actual blood, or perhaps a red (blood) color, resulting from these events. Interestingly, the term "Red-tide" represents a chemical imbalance in the sea, and this causes a red color in the water of the ocean. This "red-tide" also kills vast amounts of sea-life.

- **Revelation 8:10-11:** *"The third angel sounded his trumpet, and a **great star**, blazing like a torch, fell from the sky on a third of the rivers and on the springs of water – the name of the star is Wormwood. **A third of the waters turned bitter** and many people died from the waters that had become bitter."* Again, this "great star", which "fell from the sky", could represent a meteor or perhaps another ICBM re-entering the atmosphere. "Wormwood" (Greek: apsinthos), means a bitter, often poisonous herb of drug that will pollute a third of the fresh water on earth.

- **Revelation 8:12:** *"The fourth angel sounded his trumpet, and a third of the sun was struck, a third of the moon, and a third of the stars, so that a third of them turned dark. **A third of the day was without light, and also a third of the night.**"* All natural light will now be diminished by a third. Also we see that the sunlight during the day will be reduced by one-third and the night will be one-third darker. It seems apparent that the pollution circulating the earth from the previous judgments, whether from nuclear detonations and/or meteors and/or volcanoes, will all serve to darken the amount of sunlight significantly.

- **Revelation 9:1-11:** *"The fifth angel sounded his trumpet and I saw a star that had fallen from the sky to the earth. The star was given the key to the shaft to the abyss. When he opened the abyss, smoke rose from it like the smoke from a gigantic furnace. The sun and the sky were darkened by the smoke from the abyss. **And out of the smoke locusts came down upon the earth and were given power like that of scorpions of the earth.** They were told not to harm the grass of the earth or any plant or tree, but only those people who did not have the seal of God on their foreheads. They were not given the power to kill them, but only to torture them for five months. And the agony they suffered was like that of the sting of a scorpion when it strikes a man. During those days men will seek death, but will not find it; they will long to die, but death will elude them. The locusts looked like horses prepared for battle. On their heads they wore something like crowns of gold, and their faces resembled human faces. Their hair was like women's hair, and their* *teeth were like lions teeth. They had breastplates of iron and the sound of their wings was like the thundering of many horses and chariots rushing into battle. They had tails and stings like scorpions, and in their tails they had power to torment people for five months. They had a king over them the angel of the abyss, whose name in Hebrew is Abaddon, and in Greek, Apolyon."* The "star" mentioned here seems to refer to a person, rather than a literal star or meteor. Additionally, this "star", referred to as a "he", is given the key to the abyss. Scripture from Isaiah 14: 12 give us the reference that Satan is the fallen star from heaven, *"How you have fallen from heaven, O morning star, son of the dawn, you have been cast down to the earth."* This "abyss", or "bottomless pit", (Greek: abyssos), is the abode of demons, according to Luke 8:31. The Greek word is found seven times in Revelation (9:1, 2, 11; 11:7; 17:8; 20:1, 3), and from these references, it may be concluded that the abyss is the place of detention of demons, or "wicked angels".

There are diverse opinions on the meaning of these creatures – as to whether they are supernatural, mutant locusts specifically created for this judgment or whether they symbolize some modern equipment such as helicopters containing a form of chemical warfare. The humans who were harmed by these Locusts are said to be *"...only those people who did not have the seal of God on their foreheads."* The reference to the "sealed" represent the 144,000 witnesses for Christ as described in Revelation 7. According to 2 Timothy 2:19, *"Nevertheless, God's solid foundation stands firm, sealed with this inscription: The Lord knows those who are his..."*

• **Revelation 9:13:** *"The sixth angel sounded his trumpet, and I heard a voice coming from the horns of the* *golden alter that is before God. It is said to the sixth angel who had the trumpet, 'Release the four angels who are bound at the great river Euphrates.' **And the four angels who had been kept ready for this very hour and day and month and year were released to kill a third of mankind.** The number of the mounted troops was two hundred million."* An additional one-third of mankind has now been killed. Earlier, in Rev. 6: 8, one-fourth of the population was destroyed. These two judgments alone account for approximately one-half of the world's population. There is also additional widespread destruction and death from the other various judgments, thus the number of human deaths would far exceed half of the human population, just during the judgments seen thus far. The reference to 200 million troops here is assumed to come from the East, as the angels of verse 14 were bound at the Euphrates River. This idea is confirmed with Rev. 16: 12. For the first time in history, there will be a full scale invasion of the west by the Orient. China alone can now mount an army of > 200 million men consisting of the armed and organized militia. Rev. 16: 12 indicates that there will be a full mobilization of "the Kings of the East".

- **Revelation 11:15, 19:** *"The seventh angel sounded his trumpet, and there were loud voices in heaven, which said 'The kingdom of the world has become the kingdom of our Lord and of his Christ, and he will reign forever and forever.' Then God's temple in heaven was opened and **within his temple was seen the ark of his covenant.** And there came flashes of lightening, rumblings, peals of thunder, an earthquake and a great hailstorm."* With this trumpet judgment, we can now see that the last judgments are about to take place, and the people of God, surrounding his throne, can now see the long awaited

Kingdom of God, ready to be established. This caused them to sing praises. Verses 15-18 show that those in heaven worshiping God are anticipating both the ending of the "wrath" and the beginning of his "reign". Verse 19 also reveals the presence of the ark. Believing Jews knew that this ark was where God dealt with their sin and separation from Him. The ark being revealed here, indicates that God will be faithful to His covenant of forgiveness with those who accept the message of Christ and salvation. The chapter ends with flashes of lightening, thunder and an earthquake, a warning that God's final judgments are now underway for those who reject the Messiah.

- **Revelation 16:1-2:** *"Then I heard a loud voice from the temples saying to the seven angels, 'Go, pour out the seven bowls of God's wrath on the earth.' The first angel went and poured out his bowl on the land, and ugly and painful sores broke out on the people who had the mark of the beast and worshiped his image."* The "loud" or "great" voice is clearly that of God. Those who have received the "mark of the beast" have already cast their allegiance with the Antichrist and thus, have formally turned from God. The book of Revelation made it clear that this allegiance was to be irreversible (Rev. 14: 9-10 and Rev. 19: 20). The "image" which the Antichrist forces people to worship is described in Rev. 13: 14-15. It is possible that the mark of the beast, presumably an implantable microchip, may cause an "allergic" type of reaction in the body causing these sores, or these sores could simply be of "supernatural" origins.

- **Revelation 16:3:** *"The second angel poured out his bowl on the sea, and it turned into blood like that of a dead man, and every living thing in the sea died."* We now see a similar but more extensive judgment as compared with

Revelation 8: 8-9, where only a third of the sea became blood and only a third of the sea-life was killed. Now, following this second bowl judgment, the entire sea turns to "blood" and every living thing in the sea is dead. Just as Jesus described in Matthew 24, like a woman in labor, the judgments become faster and more severe.

• **Revelation 16:4-7:** *"The third angel poured out his bowl on the **rivers and springs of water, and they became blood.** Then I heard the angel in charge of the waters say: 'You are just in these judgments, you who are and who were, the Holy One, because you have so judged; for they have shed the blood of your saints and prophets, and you have given them blood to drink as they deserve.' And I heard the alter respond: 'Yes, Lord God Almighty, true and just are your judgments.'"* At this point in the Tribulation, there is no drinkable fresh water. Verse 6 tells us why the judgment has been inflicted upon earth, *"for they have shed the blood of your saints and prophets, and you have given them blood to drink as they deserve."* As the saints are worthy of rest and reward, those that are wicked and turn against God are worthy of judgment. The persecution of the "saints", during the Tribulation, including the mass slaughter of those refusing to worship the Antichrist and/or refusing to take the "mark of the beast" will be like no other time in history. Christ himself describes this as a time like no other time ever before (or after) on earth (Matt. 24: 21).

Who are "The Saints"? Romans 1:6-7: *"And you also are among those who are called to belong to Jesus Christ. To all in Rome who are loved by God and called to be saints: Grace and peace to you from God our Father and from the Lord Jesus Christ."* Here we see that all Christian are "saints", in that they are "set apart" to God and are being made increasing "holy" by the Holy Spirit. A similar message is given in 1 Corinthians 1: 2: *"Unto the church of God which is at Corinth, to them that are sanctified in Christ Jesus, called to be saints, with all that in every place call upon the name of Jesus Christ our Lord..."* From these two scriptures we can see that every true believer in Christ is considered a saint in the eyes of God.

- **Revelation 16:8-9:** *"The fourth angel poured out his bowl on the sun, and **the sun was given power to scorch people with fire**. They were **seared by the intense heat** and they cursed the name of God, who had control over these plagues, but they refused to repent and glorify him."* This scripture represents another area in which the scenario described could result from massive nuclear detonations, resulting in complete loss of the ozone layer and resulting from this – a massive amount of ultraviolet solar radiation, which now unshielded would enter the atmosphere. This scenario, presumably occurring after the nuclear winter would cause intense heat and deadly skin lesions. On the other hand, this could simply represent a divine intervention as issued by God, without a "man-made" cause.

- **Revelation 16:10-11:** *"The fifth angel poured out his bowl on the throne of the beast, and **his kingdom was plunged into darkness**. Men gnawed their tongues in agony and cursed the God of heaven because of their pains and their sores, **but they refused to repent** of what they had done."* Here, the "throne" of the beast and his "kingdom" represents, at a minimum, the area of the revived Roman Empire, but quite possibly the entire earth, depending upon what is meant by "his Kingdom". Revelation 13:7 indicates that the Antichrist will have *"authority over every tribe, people, language and nation."* This same darkness happened to Egypt during the plagues – the whole land was enveloped in darkness so oppressive that Moses said you could actually feel it. This darkness may allow for the events described in the next verse to take place.

- **Revelation 16:12-16:** *"The sixth angel poured out his bowl on the great river **Euphrates and its water was dried up to prepare the way for the kings of the East.** Then I saw three evil spirits that looked like frogs; they came out of the mouth of the dragon, out of the mouth of the beast and out of the mouth of the false prophet. They are spirits of demons performing miraculous signs, and they go out to **the kings of the whole world, to gather them for the battle** on the great day of God Almighty."* Interestingly, Turkey now has a dam which can completely dry the Euphrates River, allowing for completion of this verse. As with other judgments, the drying of the Euphrates could be simply a divine act by God, or it could also happen by Man's actions (i.e., causing the dam to dry this river). Importantly, unclean spirits will come from the Antichrist ("beast"), the False Prophet and Satan (the "dragon" – Revelation 12:9, 13:1-8, 13:11-18). The purpose of this drying of the Euphrates is to allow the "kings of the east" to cross, in order to be present at the time of *"the battle on the great day of God Almighty."* The sixth trumpet judgment (Revelation 9) revealed vast armies from the east which were *preparing* to march into the middle east – now this army of > 200 million Asian troops has actually reached the banks of the Euphrates, the ancient boundary between the East and the West. These eastern troops most likely consist of China, and perhaps also include Japan, India, Korea and other countries in that region. Approximately 2,700 years ago, the Prophet Joel foresaw this day (Joel 3: 12-14), *"Let the nations be awakened, and come to the valley of Jehoshaphat (the place of*

Armageddon), for there I will sit to judge all the nations surrounding you. Multitudes, multitudes in the valley of decision; for the day of the Lord is near the valley of decision."

• **Revelation 16:17:** *"The seventh angel poured out his bowl into the air, and **out of the temple came a loud voice from the throne, saying, 'It is done!' Then there came flashes of lightening, rumblings, peals of thunder and a severe earthquake.** No earthquake like it has ever occurred since man has been on earth, so tremendous was the quake. The great city split into three parts, and the cities of the nations collapsed. God remembered Babylon the Great and gave her the cup filled with the wine of the fury of his wrath. Every island fled away and the mountains could not be found. **From the sky huge hailstones of about 100 pounds each fell upon men.** And they cursed God on account of the plague of the hail, because the plague was so terrible."* The voices, lightening and "rumblings", thunder etc., indicate that the following judgments come as express judgments from God. The cities and the mountains will disappear as the entire earth will be affected by the earthquake. This is followed by 100 pound hailstones which fall to earth.

Revelation: Additional Information and Explanations

During the descriptions given in Revelation of the various judgments during this tribulation period, there are several sections of the book which give the reader important detailed information. This information includes descriptions of the Antichrist, the False Prophet, the "two witnesses" for God, the 144,000 sealed, new believers, "The woman on the beast" and the fall of Babylon, just to name a few. Chapters 7, 11, 12, 13, 14, 17 and 18 provide this information.

144,000 Witnesses

Revelation 7:3-4: *"Do not harm the land or the sea or the trees until we put a seal on the foreheads of the servants of our God. Then I heard the number of those who were sealed: 144,000 from all the tribes of Israel"* This "sealing" of the witnesses takes place at the very beginning of the Tribulation, because it occurs prior to the various judgments. These "witnesses" will serve a very important role in terms of witnessing about Christ, and importantly, they are "sealed" or protected during the Tribulation. These are newly converted Christians. There is an obvious omission of **any discussion** of "the Church" in this section. Just as these important witnesses to Christ are being explained, and their protection during the Tribulation, there is absolutely no mention of the Church. One has to ask, if the Church was to be present during the Tribulation, why would it not be "protected" like these newly converted believers? Again, no mention of the Church here is an obvious omission. **Revelation 14** gives additional detail regarding these 144,000 people.

Revelation 14:1, 4: *"Then I looked, and there before me was the Lamb, standing on Mt Zion, and with him 144,000 who had his name and his Father's name written on their foreheads. They follow the Lamb wherever he goes. They were purchased from among men and offered as first fruits to God and the Lamb."*

Revelation 7:9, 13-14: *"After this, I looked and there before me was a great multitude that no one could count,*

from every nation, tribe, people and language, standing before the throne and in front of the Lamb. They were wearing white robes and were holding palm branches in their hands. Then one of the elders asked me, 'These in white robes – who are they and where did they come from?' I answered, 'sir, you know'. And he said, 'These are they who have come out of the great tribulation; they have washed their robes and made them white in the blood of the Lamb.'"
Here, we see the results of these 144,000 witnesses for Christ and their evangelism efforts. This "multitude" represents those who were persecuted and put to death because of their faith. This passage teaches that many Jews and Gentiles alike will be saved during the Tribulation.

The command to preach the Gospel to every nation throughout the world will also be fulfilled during this time (Matthew 24:14, 28:19-20). This concept is often confused as a requirement to be fulfilled prior to the Rapture, but this is incorrect according to these scriptures. This requirement will be fulfilled prior to the Second Coming of Christ. Revelation 14:6 informs us that the gospel will be proclaimed to the entire earth during the Tribulation; ***"Then I saw another angel flying in midair, and he had the eternal gospel to proclaim to those who live on earth – to every nation, tribe, language and people."***

The Two Witnesses

Revelation 11:3-4, 6: *"And I will give power to my two witnesses, and they will prophesy for 1,260 days, clothed in sackcloth. These are the two olive trees and the two lampstands that stand before the Lord of the earth. These men have the power to shut up the sky so that it will not rain during the time they are prophesying; and they have the* *power to turn the waters into blood...*" Who are the witnesses? The very last words of the Old Testament reveal an important prophecy: *Malachi 4:5-6, "Behold, I will send you Elijah, the prophet, before the coming of the great and dreadful day of the Lord."* The great and dreadful day of the Lord is a clear reference to the last half of the Tribulation, thus Elijah (2 Kings 2:11) will come prior to this period – the first half of the Tribulation. The other witness is felt to be either Enoch (Genesis 5:22, 24; Hebrews 11:5-6), because he was previously "raptured" or Moses. The fact that Enoch and Elijah both did not die, but were "translated" into Heaven, suggests that the two witnesses could actually be these two figures. However, both Moses and Elijah were with Jesus during the Transfiguration (Matthew 17), and both Moses and Elijah had previously performed miracles similar to the miracles which will be produced during the Tribulation. These scriptures would suggest that Moses and Elijah would serve as the two witnesses during the Tribulation.

Regardless of the identity of second witness (the first witness is generally assumed to be Elijah), these two prophets will have an impact in saving many souls as described in Revelation 7. They will serve God in several ways: 1) to provide dramatic witnesses for Christ, 2) to present the Christian gospel to the world, and 3) to "unblind" the nation of Israel to the truth.

Ultimately, these two witnesses will make enemies of the Antichrist and those who choose to reject Christ during the first half of the Tribulation (1,260 days). For reasons known only to God, the Antichrist will be allowed to overcome and kill the two prophets once they have "finished their testimony" (Revelation 11:7). Then the unsaved world will refuse to bury their bodies, and for three and one-half days the world will see their dead bodies, as described in Revelation 11:9: *"For three and a half days men from every people, tribe, language and nation will gaze on their bodies and refuse them burial."*

Here, we have another scripture which could only apply to our current generation, because television is now available with satellite technology existing in the entire world. This development in technology now allows for minute to minute news traveling to the entire world. This availability of televised news which reaches every corner of the globe now permits literal fulfillment of this prophecy. Revelation 3:11-12 confirms this: *"But after the three and a half days a breath of life from God entered them, and they stood on their feet, and terror struck those who saw them. They heard a voice from Heaven saying to them, 'Come up here.' And they went up to heaven in a cloud, while their enemies looked on."* Again, the entire world will be watching as these two figures ascend to heaven. God again reveals his supremacy over the Antichrist and any events that can happen on earth.

A Brief Review of Israel's History (Revelation 12)

Revelation 12 contains a brief review of Israel's past history, followed by a brief look at the future.

Revelation 12:1-5: These verses describe a *"woman, clothed with the sun and the moon under her feet, and upon her head a crown of 12 stars; And she being with child cried, travailing in birth, and pained to be delivered. And there appeared another wonder in heaven; and behold a great red dragon, having seven heads and ten horns, and seven crowns upon his heads...and the dragon stood before the woman who was about to give birth, so that he might devour her child, so that he might devour her child the moment that it was born. She gave birth to a son, a male* *child who will rule all the nations...and the child was snatched up to God and his throne."* The woman described here is Israel, as she is seen by Joseph in Genesis 37:9-10. Additionally, the child that Satan ("the dragon") tries to devour is Christ, the chosen child of Israel who, one day soon "rule all nations". It is Christ who Satan has tried to have killed throughout the Bible.

Revelation 12:6: *"And the woman fled into the desert to a place **prepared for her by God, where she might be taken care of for 1,260 days.** "* This scripture supports the other reference which gives similar information as the scriptures in Matthew 24:15-20, Daniel 8:21, 9:27 and 12:1, all of which describe the people of Israel fleeing away from Jerusalem at the mid-point of the Tribulation. Because of the repetitive nature of this prophecy it seems evident that it is of great importance. This also serves as another indication that this "woman" indeed represents Israel, and again reveals the "Great Tribulation" period as being three and one-half years.

Revelation 12:9: *"And the great dragon was cast out, **that ancient serpent called the devil, or Satan, who leads the whole world astray.** "* This verse clearly identifies the dragon as Satan. The "ancient serpent" makes a reference to Satan in the Garden of Eden and the temptation of Eve. The title "devil" comes from the Greek word "diabolos" which means "accuser" or "slanderer". The name "Satan" comes from Hebrew and means "adversary".

Revelation 12:13-14: *"When the dragon saw that he had been hurled to earth, he pursued the woman who had given birth to the male child. **The woman was given two wings of a great eagle, so that she might fly to the place prepared for her in the desert, where she would be taken care of for***

a time, times and half a time." Again, we see another reference to the people of Israel fleeing Jerusalem at the midpoint of the Tribulation (see Revelation 12:9). The fact that "time, times and half a time" is equivalent to three and one-half years, or 1,260 days is seen in Revelation 12:9.

Noteworthy in this section of Revelation, where the history of the nation of Israel is given (with emphasis on the Tribulation), there is no reference to the Church. It seems a striking exclusion, particularly between verses 5-6 where the scripture goes historically, from the birth of Christ to the mid-point of the Tribulation without any pause or reference to the Church. This underscores the idea that; a) the Tribulation is a dispensation period in which the 70th "week" of Daniel is fulfilled specifically for Israel, and b) the Church is not mentioned, particularly in areas which would seem fully applicable to the Church. The fact that there is no mention of the Church, again, bolsters the concept that the Church will not be present on earth during the Tribulation.

The Antichrist and the False Prophet

Revelation 13 summarizes information relating specifically to both the Antichrist and the False Prophet. The Antichrist is referred to as "the beast". This "beast", or the Antichrist, emerges from the sea, as referenced in **Revelation 17:15**, *"The waters which you saw...are peoples and multitudes and nations and tongues."* In Bible terms or usage, the ocean typically represents the unbelieving nations (1). **Isaiah 57:20:** *"The wicked are like the troubled sea, when it cannot rest, who waters cast up mire and dirt."* Here, we are being told that the Antichrist will rise up from this chaos of "the nations". Some scholars see the "waters" as representing the Mediterranean area, and thus feel that the beast will arise from this one of the countries surrounding the Mediterranean.

Revelation 13:1: *"And I saw a beast coming out of the sea. He had ten horns and seven heads, with ten crowns on his horns, and on each head a blasphemous name."* This beast has an identical description in Revelation 17:3, *"a scarlet beast that was covered with blasphemous names and has seven heads and ten horns."* (Also see Daniel 7:24 for an identical description of the ten horns).

Revelation 17:9: *"This calls for a mind with wisdom. The seven heads are seven hills on which the woman sits. They are also seven kings. Five have fallen, one is and the other has not yet come; but when he does come, he must remain for a little while. The beast who once was, and now is not, is an eighth king. He belongs to the seven and is going to his destruction."* The "five" that have "fallen" represent the five world empires which, at their time, had gained "world-empire" status. The five who had ceased to exist before John's time were: *Egypt, Assyria. Babylon, Medo-Persia, and Greece.* The "one is" represents the "world-empire" at the time of John, or Rome. *"...and the other is not yet come"* refers to the revival of the Roman empire at the end of the age, *"and when he does come, he must remain for a little while."*

From the explanation given, we can see that these seven heads represent seven "kings" or "world empires" and these seven are seen as being successive, as they have a distinct order of appearance. The phrase, *"He must remain for a little while"* indicates the brief period for the final gentile kingdom, or the Antichrist's reign (seven years) as compared to the previous empires.

The final phrase in this scripture, *"The beast who once was, and now is not, is an eighth king. He belongs to the seven and is going to his destruction"* describes the Antichrist, who has been referred to as "the beast", thus it stands to reason that this "eighth king" is a reference to the Antichrist. Additionally, *"He belongs to the seven"* references the fact that the Antichrist comes from the seventh gentile kingdom or world empire, which is in the form of the Revived Roman Empire.

The Ten Horns: The Last World Empire

The Ten Horns: (Revelation 13:1, 17:12-14; Daniel 7:24). The ten horns are explained both in Daniel 7:24 and Revelation 17:12. Revelation 17:12: *"The ten horns you saw are ten kings who have not yet received a kingdom, but who for one hour will receive authority as kings along with the beast. They will make war against the Lamb but the Lamb will overcome them because he is the Lord of lords and King of Kings."* In Daniel 7:24 we see the following; *"The ten horns are ten kings who will come from this kingdom. After them another king will arise different from the earlier ones...He will speak against the Most High and oppress his saints...His saints will be handed over to him for a time, times and half a time."* Clearly, the ten horns, representing the ten kings, are **not** a succession of kings, as we saw with the seven heads, but these kings will exist at the **same time**. These ten will receive authority **"for one hour"...**as kings **"along with the beast"**. These kings will "come from this kingdom", the last gentile kingdom/world empire. Therefore it is obvious that this last world empire will consist of **Ten Kings or a Ten Member Ruling Body**. Also we see from Revelation 17:13, *"They have one purpose and they will give their power and authority to the* *beast.*" From these passages we have the information that not only will these ten "kings" form the last world empire, but their sole purpose will be to support the Antichrist.

This last empire will immediately precede the Second Coming of Christ because it is the very kingdom that is destroyed by Christ at the time of the Second Coming. Daniel 2:44, *"In the time of those kings, the God of heaven will set up a kingdom that will never be destroyed, nor will it be left to another people. It will crush all those kingdoms and bring them to an end, but will itself endure forever."*

Daniel 7:26 references the fate of the Antichrist and this last world empire: *"But the court will sit, and his power will be taken away and completely destroyed forever. Then the sovereignty, power and greatness of the kingdoms under the whole heaven will be handed over to the saints, the people of the Most High. His kingdom will be an everlasting kingdom, and all rulers will worship and obey him."*

Another reference indicating that this last kingdom will serve as the final gentile world empire, just before the return of Christ, is found in Revelation 17:14, *"They will make war against the Lamb, but the Lamb will overcome them because he is the Lord of lords and King of kings."* This scripture tells us that the Antichrist will reign right up until Christ returns and subsequently destroys the Antichrist.

Revelation 13:2: *"The beast I saw represented a leopard, but had feet like a bear and a mouth like that of a lion. The dragon gave the beast his power and his throne and great authority."* This description of the Antichrist (leopard, bear and lion), as working in concert with the ten kings represents the fact this final world empire will have all of the characteristics of the previous world empires as described in Daniel 7:4-6. In other words, the Antichrist will represent the embodiment of all previously beastly governments of man that has ruled the world. In addition, this last world empire will have received power and authority from Satan.

Revelation 13:4: *"Men worshiped the dragon which gave power unto the beast, and they worshipped the beast saying, 'Who is like the beast? Who can make war against him?'"* This final form of apostasy is not only the worship of some pagan deity but the actual worship of Satan himself, who seeks to be "like God" (Isaiah 14: 14). Because men worship Satan, they also worship the Antichrist ("the beast") who rules over the revived Roman Empire. He (the Antichrist) is Satan's substitute for Christ. The point in history where this takes place is obviously the Tribulation, when the Antichrist takes control of the last world empire.

The Beast Out of the Earth (The False Prophet): Revelation 13:11-18

Revelation 13:11-12: *"Then I saw another beast, coming out of the earth. He had two horns like a lamb, but he spoke like a dragon.* ***He exercised all the authority of the first beast on his behalf, and made the earth and its inhabitants worship the first beast,*** *whose fatal head wound had been healed."* The fact that this second beast comes from the earth often leads to much discussion. Some scholars believe that the "earth" represents Israel, or the Holy Land, and thus the False Prophet would come from the Holy Land, and would therefore be a Jew. There is precedence for the term "earth" or "land" symbolizing the land that belongs to Israel. There is no consensus on this point however, and there remains speculation as to what this means.

More significant perhaps is the phrase: ***"Two horns like a lamb"*** which indicates that the False Prophet will appear gentle like a lamb, and having a religious personification, however he will speak *"...like a dragon"*, which is a reference to Satan's influence and motivation behind his power. This verse also indicates that this False Prophet will work along with the Antichrist, and he will force the whole world to worship the Antichrist.

The scriptural phrase *"...whose fatal head wound had been healed"* seems to indicate a direct reference to the first beast (the Antichrist). From this particular scripture one could assume that the Antichrist will, at some point during the Tribulation appear to suffer a fatal head wound and will appear to be "resurrected" from this head wound. Revelation 13: 3 states that one of the heads *"appeared"* to have this wound, suggesting a deception by the Antichrist.

This scripture could **also** indicate that the "revived" Roman Empire, from which the Antichrist initially rules, has been "healed" or revived. In this case, the interpretation would see the Antichrist as the symbol representing the revived Roman Empire, and the executor of the Empire's power and rule. Here, the interpretation also involved the idea that the fatal head wound represents the fall of the original Roman Empire, yet now has been "healed" by the rise of the Antichrist and his role as leader of this empire. These are the two primary interpretations of this passage. However, the scriptural references regarding this apparent head wound throughout Revelation 13 seem to indicate that the Antichrist, as a single individual will appear to suffer this fatal head wound, and will subsequently be "healed" via a "miracle". Several scholars have pointed out the possibility that the Antichrist will indeed be killed, but the seeming "miracle" of his "resurrection" actually represents the idea that Satan will indwell the Antichrist at this moment of "resurrection".

Revelation 13:13-15: *"And he performed great and miraculous signs, even causing fire to come down from heaven to earth in full view of men. Because of the signs he was given power to do on behalf of the first beast, he deceived the inhabitants of the earth. He ordered them to set up an image in honor of the first beast who was wounded by the sword and yet lived. He was given power to give breath to the image of the first beast, so that it could speak and cause all who refused to worship the image to be killed."*

Several identifying characteristics regarding the false prophet are revealed with the passage above. First, he performs *"great and miraculous signs"* such as making fire come from the sky to the earth in sight of onlookers. Through these types of signs, the False Prophet will be able to deceive most men. Jesus specifically warned of this in Matt. 24: 23-25:

> **"At that time if anyone says to you, 'Look, here is the Christ!' or 'There he is!' do not believe it. For false Christs and false prophets will appear and perform great signs and miracles to deceive even the elect – if that were possible. See, I have told you ahead of time. So if anyone tells you, 'There he is, out in the desert', do not go out or, 'Here he is, in the inner rooms', do not believe it. For as lightening that comes from the east is visible even in the west, so will be the coming of the Son of Man."**

In this passage, Jesus makes one point very clear: The **only** way Christ will appear again on earth will be in the dramatic manner described – visible by everyone in the entire world. The Antichrist, by contrast, as only a man, will gradually rise to power in an unremarkable manner. This one of the many ways that believers living during the Tribulation will be able to avoid the deception of the Antichrist.

"He was given power to give breath to the image of the first beast, so that it could speak and cause all who refused to worship the image to be killed." In a manner similar to that of Nebuchadnezzar, the False Prophet will set up an image of the Antichrist and demand that people worship this image. This image may be a specific representation of the Antichrist, but it could also be some sort of a symbol representing the Antichrist's power and rule. It seems that this image will become the center of the false worship that will take place during the Tribulation. The image of this idol is mentioned three times in this chapter alone and seven more times throughout the book of Revelation (Revelation 14:9, 14:11, 15:2, 16:2, 19:20 and 20:4).

The fact that this image will appear to "breathe" seems to indicate that the image will have the appearance of life because of this "breathing". The image is further described as being able to speak. Both the "breathing" and "speaking" could easily be accomplished by the techniques of movie making and special effects. This most likely represents part of the "great and miraculous" signs which Jesus warned against in Matthew 24. The absolute authority that the Antichrist and the False Prophet have is such that they will have the power to kill those who refuse such worship.

The Mark of the Beast

Revelation 13:16-17: *"He also forced everyone, small and great, rich and poor, free and slave, to receive a mark on his right hand or on his forehead, so that no one could buy or sell unless he had the mark, which is the name of the* *beast or the number of his name. This calls for wisdom. If anyone has insight, let him calculate the number of the beast, for it is a man's number. His number is 666."* The Antichrist and the False Prophet will use this "Mark of the Beast" (MOTB) to force people to declare their allegiance. This MOTB will be necessary in order to complete any financial transaction, including the buying of food, gas, and any other necessity of life.

Revelation 14:9-10 clarifies that receiving the MOTB amounts to a declaration of formal rejection of Christ: *"If any man worships the beast and his image and receives the mark in his forehead, or in his hand, the same shall drink of the wine of the wrath of God, which is poured out without mixture into the cup of His indignation; and he shall be tormented with fire and brimstone in the presence of the holy angels, and in the presence of the Lamb."*

The number **666** has accounted for endless speculation regarding its meaning. In the bible, the number **6** represents humanity, thus many believe that **666** represents, in some way, man (the Antichrist) attempting to imitate the Holy Trinity of God (three **sixes** in one person). In this case, which could be considered as an "unholy trinity" the parallels are, 1) The Antichrist = counterfeit Christ, 2) Satan = counterfeit God, and 3) the False Prophet = counterfeit Holy Spirit. In some way, which is yet unknown, the number 666 will be associated with the Antichrist, and his power.

Summary of the False Prophet:

- He is motivated by Satan (Revelation 13:11).

- He leads religion and worship during the tribulation (Revelation 13:12-15).

- He has unlimited authority (Revelation 13:12).

- He performs signs and miracles (Revelation 13:13).

- He forces people to worship the Antichrist (Revelation 13:12).

- He forces worship of an "idol" or the "image" of the Antichrist (Revelation 13:14).

- He deceives the population (Revelation 13:14).

- He kills all who refuse to worship the Antichrist and his image (Revelation 13:15).

- He controls commerce and all who can buy or sell via implementation of the Mark of the Beast, (Revelation 13:16).

The Woman on the Beast

Chapter 17 describes several important details regarding the false religion in existence at the time of the Tribulation, beginning with **Revelation 17:1-6:**

"One of the seven angels who had the seven

*bowls came and said to me, 'Come, **I will** **show you the punishment of the great pros-** **titute,** who sits on many waters. With her the kings of the earth committed adultery and the inhabitants of the earth were intoxicated with the wine of her adulteries.' Then the angel carried me away in the spirit into a desert. There **I saw a woman sitting on a** **scarlet beast that was covered with blasphe-** **mous names and had seven heads and ten** **horns.** The woman was dressed in purple and scarlet, and was glittering with gold, precious stones and pearls. She held a golden cup in her hand filled with abdominal things and the filth of her adulteries. This title was written on her forehead:*

Mystery
Babylon the Great
The Mother of Prostitutes
And of the Abominations of the Earth

I saw that the woman was drunk with the blood of the saints, the blood of those who bore testimony to Jesus."

Biblically, the terms "whore", "harlot", and "adultery" are frequently used to symbolize a spiritual departure from God, false teachings and departure from His truth. The words indicate the existence of a religion that is counterfeit to God's word (Isaiah 1: 21; Ezekiel 16: 8, 17; Nahum 3: 4 and James 4: 4). Throughout the history of Israel, every time the people strayed from faith, it was because of false teachings which ultimately led to a departure from God's word.

The harlot mentioned in Revelation 17 is associated with Babylon – the ancient city which was consumed with false religions, occult practices, immorality, arrogance, astrology, sorcery, and witchcraft. The gold cup is filled with "abdominal things" representing these corrupt and perverse teachings. The fact that she was "drunk with the blood of the saints" reveals the persecution of those believing in the true word of God. The primary message is that *religious* Babylon would be revived to control the last great world empire. For the first half of the Tribulation, this false religion will have great power and influence over the revived Roman Empire and will be led by the False Prophet and the Antichrist.

Revelation 17:15-17: *"Then the angel said to me, 'the waters you saw, where the prostitute sits are peoples, multitudes, nations and languages. The beast and the ten horns will hate the prostitute. They will bring her to ruin and leave her naked; they will eat her flesh and burn her with fire. For God has put it into their hearts to accomplish his purpose by agreeing to give the beast their power to rule until God's words are fulfilled. The woman you saw is the great city that rules over the kings of the earth.'"* In this passage, we again see the reference that this false religion will encompass the whole world. As seen in Chapter 13, the False Prophet will use this religion to force people to worship the Antichrist. In the middle of the Tribulation, the Roman Antichrist has gained enough power that he no longer needs the support of the False Prophet and the false religious system, and in turn, proclaims himself as God in the Temple; *"The beast and the ten horns will hate the prostitute. They will bring her to ruin..."* This world church is destroyed in favor of a world "religion" strictly honoring/worshiping the Antichrist.

The Fall of Babylon

Revelation 18:1-3: *"After this I saw another angel coming down from heaven. He had great authority, and the earth was illuminated by his splendor. With a mighty voice he shouted: 'Fallen! Fallen is Babylon the Great! She has become a home for demons and a haunt for every evil spirit, a haunt for every unclean and detestable bird.'"*

Revelation 18:9-11: *"When the kings of the earth who committed adultery with her and shared her luxury see the smoke of her burning, they will weep and mourn over her. Terrified at her torment, they will stand far off and cry: 'Woe! Woe, O great city, O Babylon, city of power! In one hour your doom has come!' The merchants of the earth will mourn over her because no one buys their cargoes any more."*

Revelation 18:17-18: *"In one hour such great wealth has been brought to ruin. Every sea captain, and all who travel by trip, the sailors, and all who earn their living from the sea, will stand far off. When they see the smoke of her burning, they will exclaim, 'Was there ever a city like this great city?'"*

The exact location of this city is generally considered as one of two possibilities: 1) the city is literally a rebuilt Babylon, in Iraq, and, 2) a reference to Babylon as representing Rome. The reference to Rome is based partially on the descriptions of the seven mountains (historically, Rome has been described as the city of seven hills – even indicated as such in coins which use this reference) as given in Revelation 17: 9. The description of the "woman" arrayed in purple and scarlet is seen in association with the apparel and the trappings of the officials in the Roman Catholic and

Greek Orthodox churches. Regardless of the location of the city, it is clear that it will be destroyed "in one hour" and the burning of this city indicates the fall of its political and economic might, and the "kings" of the earth mourn over this destruction.

A Glimpse of Heaven and the Second Coming of Jesus Christ

Revelation 19:1-3: *"After this I heard what sounded like the roar of a great multitude in heaven shouting: 'Hallelujah! Salvation and glory and power belong to our God, for true and just are his judgments. He has condemned the great prostitute who corrupted the earth by her adulteries. He has avenged on her the blood of his servants.'"*

Revelation 19:7-8: *"Let us rejoice and be glad and give him glory!* **For the wedding of the Lamb has come, and his bride has made herself ready. Fine linen, bright and clean, was given her to wear. (Fine linen stands for the righteous acts of the saints.)"**

Recall the earlier descriptions of the bride of Christ as representing the Church and the marriage customs at that time: First, the marriage was arranged and planned for a future time. Second, when the couple was ready (either from reaching the appropriate age or financial preparation etc.), the groom would go to the home of the bride and escort her to the house that he had prepared for them to live. Finally, after this, the consummating event would occur – the wedding feast. As we see again, Christ is the bridegroom and the raptured Church is the bride. The fact that this scene takes place in heaven indicates that the Church has been residing in heaven during the tribulation period.

Ephesians 5: 26-27 informs us that Christ has given us His word as a means of cleansing, in order for Him to bring us into His presence as a pure and holy bride without blemish. As we know, the term "saints" represent all believers in Christ. The Church is now arrayed in *"fine linen, bright and clean."* This cleansing of the Church would only occur after the bema judgment, which is yet another "event" which will take place in Heaven prior to the Second Coming. This represents yet another argument against the post-Tribulation Rapture because with a post-Tribulation Rapture scenario, there would be no time for the wedding and the bema judgment to have taken place.

Revelation 19:9: *"Then the angel said to me, 'Write: Blessed are those who are invited to the wedding supper of the Lamb!' And he added. 'These are the **true words of God.**' "* In verses 7-9 a distinction is made between the "bride", which represents the Church and those who are "invited" to attend, presumably saints from previous ages. The idea that these are the *"true words of God"* is repeated on two additional occasions, in Revelation 21:5 and Revelation 22:6. These three occasions specifically state that these **words** themselves are to be taken as true and trustworthy – again reinforcing the literal nature of these words. This is in contrast to **Daniel 2:45:** *"The great God has shown the king what will take place in the future. **The dream is true and the interpretation is trustworthy.**"* As the verse in Daniel describes, the dream required interpretation and it was deemed as trustworthy and true. In three similar passages in Revelation, a specific point was made that the very **words** themselves are trustworthy and true; another clue that these words are to be taken literally – just as written.

Revelation 19:10: *"At this I fell at his feet to worship him. But he said to me, 'Do not do it! I am a fellow servant with* *you and with your brothers who hold to the testimony of Jesus. Worship God!* **For the testimony of Jesus is the spirit of prophecy.**'" The last statement regarding the testimony of Jesus as the spirit of prophecy indicates that the basis of prophecy revolves around Jesus. Jesus is not only the major theme of the scriptures but He is also the major focus of prophecy. The prophecy around Jesus should serve as a powerful motivating force for believers to gain perspective and to witness during the last days.

Revelation 19:11, 13, 14: *"I saw heaven standing open and there before me was a white horse, whose rider is called Faithful and True. He is dressed in a robe dipped in blood, and his name is the Word of God.* **The armies of heaven were following him, riding on white horses and dressed in fine linen, white and clean."** The return of Jesus will be exactly as described in Acts 1:8-11, Revelation 1:7-8, Zechariah 14:2-4, Matthew 24:29-31, and Daniel 7:13. Approximately 2,000 years ago the disciples watched as Christ ascended into a cloud. This scripture indicates that at the Second Coming, Christ will be seen by the world descending, through the clouds, physically. According to Zechariah 14:4-8, at the time of the Second Coming, Jesus feet will actually touch the earth at the Mount of Olives, at which time a massive earthquake will split the Mount of Olives. A fault line has been discovered in this area. These events are in stark contrast with the descriptions given for the Rapture of the Church. Matthew 24:27-31 also gives detailed and consistent information regarding the Second Coming of Christ, and indicates that the entire world will witness this event – another stark contrast with the descriptions given for the events of the Rapture.

Revelation 19:19-21: *"Then I saw the beast and the kings of the earth and their armies gathered together to make war* *against the rider of the horse and his army. But the beast was captured and with him the False Prophet who had performed the miraculous signs on his behalf. With these signs he had deluded those who had received the mark of the beast and worshiped his image. The two of them were thrown alive into the fiery lake of burning sulfur. The rest of them were killed with the sword that came out of the mouth of the rider on the horse, and all the birds gorged themselves on their flesh."* Here, the Antichrist and the False Prophet are now dealt with by Jesus, as they are cast into the lake of fire. The unsaved that have died are taken to Hades, specifically (place of "torments") for the purpose of awaiting their final judgment (Rev. 20).

The 1,000 Year Reign of Christ on Earth

Revelation 20:1-3: *"And I saw an angel coming down out of heaven, having the key to the abyss and holding in his hand a great chain. He seized the dragon, that ancient serpent, who is the·devil, or Satan, and bound him for a thousand years. He threw him into the abyss, and locked and sealed it over him, to keep him from deceiving the nations anymore until the thousand years were ended. After that, he must be set free for a short time."*

The key message from this scripture is the fact that for this 1,000 year period, Satan will be "bound" and unable to influence mankind for this length of time. The Messianic Kingdom was promised throughout the Old Testament prophecies as a period of universal peace and righteousness.

The book of Revelation doesn't give much detail on this thousand year period, but there are details in the Old Testament; Zechariah 14 tells us that Jesus will rule from the city of Jerusalem. Isaiah 11:9 states that there will be justice for all and the wicked will be immediately punished. This passage also tells us that the entire world will be filled with the knowledge of God. Isaiah 2:4 tells us that there will be peace and tranquility, where men will "beat their swords into plowshares and spears into pruning hooks and learn war no more". There will be no warfare or violence. Additionally, Isaiah 11:6 and 65:20 explain that the wolf will lie down with the lamb, and a man will be a child when he's a hundred years of age. Animals will live at peace with each other and longevity for man is described.

Obviously, for man to inhabit the earth following the Tribulation there will also have to be some kind of a restoration period, for the earth to be restored. This will involve an earth which is substantially different from that which endured the Tribulation. By combining the various scriptures detailing this 1,000 year period, one can see that existence on earth will be similar to the original Garden of Eden.

Revelation 20:4-5: *"I saw thrones on which were seated those who had been given authority to judge. And I saw the souls of those who had been beheaded because of their testimony for Jesus and because of the word of God. They had not worshiped the beast or his image and had not received the mark on their foreheads or their hands. They came to life and reigned with Christ a thousand years. The rest of the dead did not come to life until the thousand years were ended. This is the first resurrection."* This scripture introduces the topic of the fate of the souls of believers. Prior to the Second Coming of Christ, the souls of believers, at death, goes immediately to be with Jesus in heaven (2 Corinthians 5:8 and Philippians 1:21-23). At the time of the Rapture however, these deceased believers will reunite with their new "glorified" bodies. By contrast, the unbelievers will see their souls go to "torments" (Hades) and stay there until their bodies are resurrected from the grave – at the end of the 1,000 year period. This is considered the "second resurrection" – reserved for non-believers.

The first resurrection occurs in 4 phases: 1) the first phase: Jesus resurrection (1 Corinthians 15:20-25), 2) the second phase: The Rapture of the Church (for all living and deceased believers from the Church Age), 3) the third phase is for Old Testament believers. This takes place after the Tribulation, when Christ returns to earth, as the scripture indicates in Daniel 12:1-2, *"At that time Michael, the great prince who protects your people, will arise. There will be a time of distress such as has not happened from the beginning of nations until then. But at that time your people – everyone whose name is found written in the book – will be delivered. Multitudes who sleep in the dust of the earth will awake..."* In addition to the Old Testament believers, this third phase includes those tribulation saints – or those who were persecuted and killed during the Tribulation, and 4) the final phase, which is reserved for those who live through the 1,000 reign of Christ – and receive their glorified bodies at the end of this 1,000 year reign.

The "thrones" referenced in Revelation 20:4 are occupied by *"those who had been given the authority to judge"*. There is no definition in Revelation 20 as to who is represented specifically. Other places in the Bible reference the fact that believers will rule over cities and even angels during the Millennium (1 Corinthians 6:2-3), and is also referenced in Revelation 22:5. This may include not only the Church, but all saints/believers including Old Testament believers.

Clearly, from Revelation 20:4, the tribulation saints are now rewarded and blessed, and are also declared to reign with Christ for the thousand year period, *"They came to life and reigned with Christ a thousand years."*

Revelation 20:7-10: *"When the thousand years are over, Satan will be released from his prison and will go out to deceive the nations in the four corners of the earth...to gather them for battle. In number they are like the sand on the seashore. They marched across the breadth of the earth and surrounded the camp of God's people, the city he loves. But fire came down from heaven and devoured them. And the devil, who deceived them, was thrown into the lake of burning sulfur, where the beast and the False Prophet had been thrown. They will be tormented day and night for ever and ever."*

At the end of the 1,000 year reign of Christ, Satan is released and immediately organizes war. He gathers those who, although living in a perfect environment, still have rebellion in their hearts. This seems to be a lesson from God; that under every scenario, from Adam and Eve through every dispensation, man will sin. Thus man's rebellion has nothing to do with his immediate environment but with his heart. Additionally, we see that man still has an active choice to make, even during this perfect environment given to him: To align with God and repent, or to align with Satan and rebel against God. However, this "rebellion" is short-lived. As soon as this rebellion forms, God strikes it down, and subsequently Satan is sent to the Lake of Fire where the Antichrist and the False Prophet have been for the past 1,000 years. The three are specifically said to reside there "day and night for ever and ever."

The Great White Throne Judgment (Revelation 20:11-15)

Revelation 20:11-15: *"Then I saw a great white throne and him who was seated on it. Earth and sky fled from his* *presence, and there was no place for them. And I saw the dead, great and small, standing before the throne, and books were opened. Another book was opened, which is the book of life. The dead were judged according to what they had done as recorded in the books...each person was judged according to what he had done. Then death and Hades were thrown into the lake of fire. The lake of fire is the second death. If anyone's name was not found written in the book of life, he was thrown into the lake of fire."* These verses tell us that "the dead, great and small" refers to all those who have rejected Christ throughout history, and are thus spiritually dead; their previous "status" while on earth is of no relevance. Jesus stated that there would be a resurrection of life and a resurrection of the "dead".

There are several other scriptural references which confirm the idea of this resurrection (John 5:24-29; Daniel 12:1-3; Revelation 20:5, 22:12; Acts 24:15). After the millennium, these "dead" will be resurrected to appear before God. The book of life refers to those who are saved and thus have eternal life. The "book of life", which is mentioned multiple times in the New Testament, contains the name of every person born into the world. When each person dies, if he has not received God's salvation, then his name is blotted out of this book. When God opens this book at this "Great White Throne Judgment", only those names of people that have received salvation through Christ will have their name written. The "dead" will not appear written in this book (Rev. 13: 8). The other books are the books of their "works". The dead are judged based upon these "works", which essentially become irrelevant because no one's works are adequate for the purpose of receiving salvation.

There are two judgments based on "works". In the case of the judgment seat of Christ (known also as the "bema" judgment), believers are judged according to their good works and rewarded (2 Corinthians 5:10-11; Matthew 16:27, 19:21, 29; Luke 14:14). The Bema platform was used in Roman days as the platform in which rewards were given to athletes. The sins of believers have already been eliminated from record because of the gift given by Christ. Their names are written in the "book of life" – the only record that matters.

By contrast, the judgment of the "dead" (The Great White Throne Judgment) is only for non-believers - those who have not had their sins washed away by the blood of Christ, and whose names are not found in the book of life. These resurrected "dead" will be judged according to their works, without the blood of Christ to purify them. Revelation 20:13 describes this judgment: *"... and each person was judged according to what he had done."* The scriptures support the notion that those who have rejected salvation through Jesus will receive different degrees of punishment, depending upon their actions while on earth (Revelation 18:3-6, 20:13; Matthew 23:14; Ecclesiastes 12:14).

Ultimately, the decision regarding the person's eternal destiny is from the book of life, and as stated in Revelation 20:15, *"If anyone's name was not found written in the book of life, he was thrown into the lake of fire."* This casting into the lake of fire is called the "second death" because it involves a permanent condemnation for all non-believers. Attempts have been made to allegorize the lake of fire into symbolic meaning. This may be, however, in Luke 16:24 we see that the rich man gave his testimony, *"I am tormented in this flame"*. Although this description was of Hades (the interim place, for non-believers souls prior to the Great White Throne Judgment), the fact that this was a literal statement, could indicate the possibility that the lake of fire could be taken literally. There are other figurative references to "fire" however, thus the exact meaning of this lake of fire is not completely clear.

The New Heaven and the New Earth

Revelation 21:1: *"Then I saw a new heaven and a new earth, for the first heaven and first earth had passed away, and there was no longer any sea."*

Revelation 21:2: *"I saw the Holy City, the new Jerusalem, coming down out of heaven from God, prepared as a bride beautifully dressed for her husband."*

In contrast to the earthly Jerusalem, this "new Jerusalem", is seen as "holy" and is seen as coming from heaven. In Revelation 3:12, we can see the prediction; ***"Him who overcomes I will make a pillar in the temple of my God. Never again will he leave it. I will write on him the name of my God and the name of the new Jerusalem, which is coming down out of heaven from my God..."*** The assumption is that New Jerusalem is the place mentioned both here and in John 14:2: ***"In my Father's house there are many rooms; if it were not so, I would have told you. I am going there to prepare a place for you. And if I go and prepare a place for you, I will come back and take you to be with me that you also may be where I am."***
New Jerusalem scripturally now appears following the 1,000 year reign of Christ and is shown as a bride. Presumably, this is where Christians will reside during the 1,000 year millennial reign and for the remainder of eternity. This idea is bolstered by the reference in Revelation 21:2, *"prepared as a bride..."* and later when John gets additional detail on this great city, Revelation 21:9-10, ***"Come I will show you the bride, the wife of the Lamb. And he carried me away in the spirit to a mountain great and high, and showed me the Holy City, Jerusalem, coming down out of heaven from God."***
This scriptural reference seems to be telling us that New

Jerusalem represents the dwelling place of the "bride" of Christ; the Church. The idea that this is where the "bride" dwells would also explain where believers reside during the millennial reign of Christ.

The inclusion of Jewish believers ultimately residing in New Jerusalem as well, is based upon the detailed description of New Jerusalem: Revelation 21:12, *"It had a great high wall with 12 gates, and 12 angels at the gates. On the 12 gates were written the names of the 12 tribes of Israel."* Further confirmation for the presence of the Church is found in Revelation 21:14, *"The wall of the city has 12 foundations, and on them were the names of the 12 apostles of the lamb."* Because we will be with Jesus forever, beginning at the time of the Rapture, it opens the possibility that believers will be able to "come and go" between their primary residing place of New Jerusalem and Earth, similar to what Jesus could do in his heavenly body.

Revelation 21:11, 21:15-27 and 22:1-5 include detailed descriptions of New Jerusalem. Just before this description and just after this detailed description we see the words in **Revelation 21: 5,** *"He who was seated on the throne said, 'I am making everything new!' Then he said, 'Write this down, for these words are trustworthy and true.'"* And Revelation 22: 6, *"The angel said to me, 'These words are trustworthy and true. The Lord, the God of the spirits of the prophets sent his angel to show his servants the things that must soon take place.'"* These statements argue for a literal interpretation of the prophecy scriptures.

Detailed descriptions of New Jerusalem include the brilliance of the various gates and walls of the city (Revelation 21:18-21), the presence of God and the light of God as lighting the city (Revelation 21:22-25), the presence of Jesus (Revelation 21:22), the purity and holiness of the city (Revelation 21:26-27), the river of the "water of life", and the "tree of life" (not mentioned since Genesis 3) bearing 12 crops of fruit; the leaves of the tree for the healing of the nations (Revelation 22:1-2), the ending of the curse, which was imposed since the time of Adam and Eve (Revelation 22:3), the presence of the God (Revelation 22:3-5), and the fact that this will last for eternity (Revelation 22:5).

Revelation 22:7: *"Behold, I come quickly; blessed is he who keeps the words of this prophecy in this book."*

Revelation 22:10: *"Then he told me, 'Do not seal up the words of the prophecy of this book, because the time is near.'"*

Revelation 22:12: *"Behold, I am coming soon! My reward is with me, and I will give to everyone according to what he has done."*

Revelation 22:20: *"He who testifies to these things says, 'Yes, I am coming soon.'"*

Verse 7 seems to link two important thoughts, 1) *"I come quickly"* and 2) *"who keeps the words of this prophecy in this book"* or to *"testify"* to the words implies an understanding of the specific words. To "keep the words of the book" and to be able to "testify" assumes that one must possess a certain level of understanding. Thus, for the generation that gains such an understanding, his coming will *"come quickly"*. Although the book was apparently to be made available for the entire church age, it has only been "kept" or understood and used in this generation. With the explosion of books and information on end time prophecy over the past several decades, it seems obvious that the information contained within has become "unsealed". This idea is consistent with Daniel 12: 4, *"But you, Daniel, close up and seal the words of the scroll until the time of the end. Many will go here and there to increase knowledge."* This was repeated in Daniel 12: 9, *"...Go your own way, Daniel, because the words are closed up and sealed until the time of the end."* One could assume from linking the scriptures Revelation and Daniel that once an understanding and usage of these prophecies takes place, then Jesus will *"come quickly"*. The concluding scripture seen in Revelation 22:20 adds to this concept, as the phrase *"He who testifies to these things"* also suggests an understanding of the scriptures. To "testify" indicates a certain understanding.

Final Instructions

Revelation 22:18: *"I warn everyone who hears the words of the prophecy of this book: If anyone adds anything to them, God will add to him the plagues described in this book. And if anyone takes away from this book of prophecy, God will take away from him his share in the tree of life and in the holy city, which are described in this book."*

There are many warnings against tampering with the word of God (Deuteronomy 4:2, 12:32; Proverbs 30:6; Revelation 1:3) but this is certainly the sternest warning. This also seems to be a warning to not add one's own interpretation to these words, which is consistent with the message from 2 Peter 1:20: *"For prophecy never had its origin in the will of man, but men spoke from God, as they were carried along by the Holy Spirit."* This scripture from Peter confirms the same message from Revelation 21:5 and 22:6, which describe that all prophecies are trustworthy and true. These scriptures all point to the requirement for a literal translation – a translation which does not require "the will of man" for interpretation.

Revelation 22:20: *"He who testifies to these things says, 'Yes I am coming soon.' Amen. Come, Lord Jesus. The Grace of the Lord Jesus be with God's people. Amen"*

CHAPTER TEN NOTES

1. Hal Lindsey. There's a New World Coming (Harvest House. 1984).

2. John F. Walvoord. The Revelation of Jesus Christ. A Commentary by John F. Walvoord (Moody Press. 1981).

ELEVEN

EZEKIEL'S PROPHECY FOR TODAY

Ezekiel 38:23: And so I will show my greatness and my holiness, and I will make myself known in the sight of many nations. Then they will know that I am the Lord.

There are several prophecies given to us by the Old Testament prophets that apply to the last days, however there are wide diversions among the scholars as to the relative timing of these prophecies. Ezekiel 36-39 gives a broad overview of Israel's history, past and future. These prophecies are important, because as we "watch" for the development of various end time events, the information given by Ezekiel is appearing specifically as written.

One cannot study the prophets, as their writings apply to our time, without a thorough study of Ezekiel 36-39. These four chapters give broad, sweeping prophecies about the nation of Israel, beginning at the time of Israel's formation as a nation, and then at the time of destruction, with the people subsequently scattered throughout the world. This prophecy was fulfilled in 70 A.D. (Ezekiel 36). Following this period of dispersion of the nation of Israel, Ezekiel made one of his most amazing prophecies - one which has been fulfilled literally. In chapter 36 and 37, the rebirth of the nation of Israel was described. In 1948, the world witnessed this miraculous fulfillment of prophecy as Israel formally became a nation once again. Following this prophecy, Ezekiel then described events destined for Israel in the "future years".

Ezekiel 36: The People of Israel Scattered Throughout the World

This chapter of Ezekiel is important for two primary reasons. First, we find yet another example of literal fulfillment of prophecy. Secondly, this chapter sets up the remaining prophetic chapters in the book of Ezekiel, as they apply to the last generation.

Ezekiel 36:16-19: *"Again the word of the Lord came to me: 'Son of man, when the people of Israel were living in their own land, they defiled it by their conduct and actions...So I poured out my wrath on them because they had shed blood in the land and because they had defiled it with their idols.* **I dispersed them among the nations, and they were scattered through the countries;** *I judged them according to their conduct and their actions.'"* This verse described the dispersion of the people of the nation of Israel, following the destruction of Jerusalem in 70 A.D. After the descriptions of this dispersion, Ezekiel gives us a hint as to what will follow: **Ezekiel 36:24** - *"For I will take you out of the nations:* **I will gather you from all the countries and bring you back into your own land.***"* This regathering of the people of the nation of Israel is given greater attention in Ezekiel 37.

Ezekiel 37: The People of Israel Regathered

Chapter 37 of Ezekiel describes the regathering of the

people of Israel, following their long exile of dispersion into the "nations". At the time of Ezekiel's writing, Israel had ceased to exist as a city. There was no place even called "Israel" nor had it existed for over 150 years. However, Ezekiel constantly referred to a future place called "Israel". In this chapter, Ezekiel is shown a valley of dry bones, which he sees coming together and then developing "tendons and flesh" followed by "skin" covering them. The Lord explained that these dry bones represent the whole house of Israel, **Ezekiel 37:11** *"Then he said to me: 'Son of man, **these bones are the whole house of Israel.** They say our bones are dried up and our hope is gone; we are cut off.'"* **Ezekiel 37:12** *"...I will bring you back to the land of Israel."* Further clarification of this is given in **Ezekiel 37:21** *"...I will take the Israelites out of the nations where they have gone. I will gather them from all around and bring them back into their own land, on the mountains of Israel."*

Over 2,500 years ago, Ezekiel detailed events which would happen in our generation. He told us of dramatic and unexpected events - events have been unprecedented in world history – the events of a nation coming together following centuries of exile yet preserving all customs and language. As we know, in 1948, following a series of meetings in the early, post-World War II era of negotiations and reforming Europe, Israel was reborn as a nation. On May 14, 1948, U.S. President Harry Truman's administration made the announcement, "The United States recognizes the provisional government as the de-facto authority of the New State of Israel." Apparently, even the name "Israel" was something that wasn't decided until the very last minute of negotiations. This represents not only a very literal fulfillment of Old Testament prophecy, but represents a prophecy that we can see occurring in our generation. These prophecies serve as another reminder that we should read and study biblical prophecy in a literal manner.

Ezekiel 38: Gog and MaGog

We have seen in chapters 36 and 37 the fulfillment of Ezekiel's prophecy concerning the nation of Israel. The dispersion of the Jews which occurred in 70 A.D. was followed centuries later by the regathering and rebirth of the nation of Israel specifically as Ezekiel predicted. The remainder of Ezekiel 38 and 39 takes us to the future, as the events described in these scriptures have not yet occurred. These prophecies describe the future events for the nation of Israel.

Ezekiel 38:1-6, *"The word of the Lord came to me: 'Son of man, set your face against* **Gog, of the land of MaGog, the chief prince of Meshech and Tubal;** *prophesy against him and say: This is what the Sovereign Lord says: I am against you, O Gog, chief prince of Meshech and Tubal. I will turn you around, put hooks in your jaws and bring you out with your whole army – your horses, your horsemen fully armed, and a great horde with large and small shields, all of them brandishing their swords.* **Persia, Cush and Put** *will be with them, all with shields and helmets, also* **Gomer with all its troops,** *and* **Beth Togarmah from the far north with all its troops** *– the many nations with you.'"* In this scripture, we can clearly see that Gog, who will be the leader of the land of MaGog, will lead many nations (including Persia, Cush, Put, Gomer and Beth Togarmah – whose identity will be discussed) into battle.

Ezekiel 38:8-9, *"After many days you will be called to arms. In future years you will invade a land that has recovered from war, whose people were gathered from many nations to the mountains of Israel, which had been desolate. They had been brought out from the nations, and now all of them live in safety. You and all your troops and the many nations with you will go up, advancing like a storm; you will be like a* *cloud covering the land."* With this passage, we can see that these nations will advance upon Israel "like a storm".

Ezekiel 38:18-23, *"This is what will happen in that day: When Gog attacks the land of Israel, my hot anger will be aroused, declares the Sovereign Lord. In my zeal and fiery wrath I declare that at that time there shall be a great earthquake in the Land of Israel...and all the people of the earth will tremble at my presence. The mountains will be overturned, the cliffs will crumble and every wall will fall to the ground. I will summon a sword against Gog on all my mountains, declares the Sovereign Lord. Every man's sword will be against his brother. I will execute judgment upon him with plague and bloodshed; I will pour down torrents of rain, hailstones and burning sulfur on him and on his troops and on the many nations with him. And so I will show my greatness and my holiness, and I will make myself known in the sight of many nations. Then they will know that I am the Lord."* At the time of this invasion, led by Gog and the countries he has assembled, we can see from the scripture that God will divinely intervene and destroy the invading forces.

Who are these countries aligned with Gog? According to evangelical scholars, these countries are relatively easy to identify in today's world. Genesis 10 contains essential information for this purpose. Genesis 10 lists the sons of Noah and where they migrated after the flood. Japheth migrated to the north from Asia Minor, beyond the Caspian and Black seas. Genesis 10: 2 lists the sons of Japheth: Gomer, MaGog, Madai, Javan, Tubul, and Meshech. The names mentioned above, in Ezekiel 38 are all sons of Japheth. The "Japhethites" became the people of the north, in the area of Rosh, which is now modern Russia. Because of these migrations of the descendants of Noah, it is clear that

Russia is being referenced in these verses of Ezekiel 38 (1). This idea is confirmed by reading **Ezekiel 39: 1-2** *"Son of man, prophesy against Gog and say: 'This is what the Sovereign Lord says: I am against you, O Gog, chief prince of Meshech and Tubal. I will turn you around and drag you along.* **I will bring you from the far north** *and send you against the mountains of Israel.' "*

Ezekiel 38:5-6 mention the other countries who will be aligned with the prince of Rosh, labeled here as Gog. The most succinct and I believe, accurate description of the remaining countries in this alliance is given by Dwight Pentecost, in "Prophecy for Today" (2):

> A great military movement under the leadership of Gog, the prince of Rosh, is described in Ezekiel 38:4: "And I will turn thee back, and put hooks in thy jaws, and I will bring thee forth, and all of thine army, horses and horsemen, all of them clothed with all sorts of armour, even a great company with bucklers and shields, all of them handling swords." Verses 5 and 6 list the allies of Russia: Persia, Ethiopia, Libya, Gomer, Togarmah, and all his bands. We have no trouble identifying Persia; we know it today as Iran, a country situated east of Palestine. But Ethiopia and Libya are used in two distinctly different senses in the Old Testament. Nations in Africa known as Ethiopia and Libya continue to the present time. But in Old Testament times there were states adjacent to Persia known as Ethiopia and Libya. When Moses fled from Egypt after slaying an Egyptian, he went into the wilderness and married an Ethiopian. He did not go

south into the African Ethiopian; he went into the Ethiopia located in the Arabian Peninsula. When Ezekiel spoke of Persia, Ethiopia and Libya, I believe he was speaking of Arab states.

From these passages, it is clear that Russia will form an alliance with these middle-eastern Arab countries, including Togarmah which is felt to represent Turkey. The common denominator with these countries is their hatred towards Israel. Interestingly, Russia has served an important, pivotal role in Iran's quest to build a nuclear facility which will permit their assembly of nuclear weapons. Israel has threatened to destroy the physical infrastructure which is being built for this purpose. These events are imminent, as Iran reaches the final stages in their quest to assemble nuclear weapons. Additionally, Iran has successfully tested missiles which could carry such nuclear warheads. Could this scenario lead to the invasion of Israel by Russia, Iran and the other countries described in these scriptures?

In summary, from these scriptures, one can see that Russia, led by a leader referred to as Gog will unite the Arab/Muslim countries and these combined military alliances will invade Israel. **Ezekiel 38:11-12** indicates that this invasion will occur for the purpose of these invading countries to *"plunder and loot"* and *"to carry off silver and gold...and to seize much plunder."* However, before this happens, just as the invaders *"attack the land of Israel"*, God will supernaturally intervene and stop this invasion. This will be done by a massive earthquake (Ezekiel 38:19-20), infighting among the invading countries (Ezekiel 38:21), disease (Ezekiel 38:22), torrential hailstones, and fire and burning sulfur (Ezekiel 38:22). Another potential scenario is that Israel could unleash their nuclear arsenal, which includes neutron bombs. The following scripture clarifies the message:

Ezekiel 39:2-6: *"...I will bring you from the far north and send you against the mountains of Israel. Then I will strike your bow from your left hand and make your arrows drop from your right hand.* **On the mountains of Israel you will fall, you and all your troops and the nations with you.** *I will give you as food to all kinds of carrion birds and to the wild animals. You will fall in the open field, for I have spoken, declares the Sovereign Lord. I will send fire on MaGog and on those who live in safety in the coastlands, and they will know that I am the Lord."*

Timing of Gog's Invasion: Interestingly, this will all occur at a time in which Israel is living in a period of relative peace and safety. According to the Lord, Gog will: *"...invade a land of unwalled villages...attack a peaceful and unsuspecting people – all living without walls and without gates and bars."* For this reason, many scholars believe it will occur at some point in the Tribulation after the Antichrist creates his "peace" covenant, thus allowing the conditions of peace that are described. Others believe that certain events preceding the Tribulation will lead to a period of relative peace, and this invasion will help trigger the Antichrist's "peace" plan. Still other scholars believe that these events occur as part of the overall series of final battles called Armageddon.

There seem to be as many theories regarding the timing of this invasion directed towards Israel, by Russia and allies, as there are Bible scholars. Each of these theories has merits, but the fact is, the specific timing of these events is unclear. The various theories include all possible scenarios for the timing: 1) before the Rapture, 2) between the Rapture and the Tribulation, and 3) during the Tribulation (differing from the beginning part of the Tribulation to the final stages of the Tribulation, as part Armageddon). Perhaps more importantly, is how current events reveal how these various alliances between Russia and the predominately Islamic nations have been forming for years. There have also been a variety of different economic and military (arms) ties between the Arab/Muslim countries and Russia that have been disclosed over the last decade. These alliances seem to be strengthening as we enter the new Millennium.

CHAPTER ELEVEN NOTES

1. John F. Walvoord. The Revelation of Jesus Christ. A Commentary by John F. Walvoord (Moody Press. 1981).

2. Dwight Pentecost. Prophecy for Today. God's Purpose and Plan for Our Future (Zondervan Publishing House. 1961).

TWELVE

FINAL PREPARATIONS

Luke 21:28: When these things begin to take place, stand up and lift your heads, because your redemption is drawing near.

Luke 21:31: Even so, when you see these things happening, you know that the Kingdom of God is near.

Jesus ended the Olivet Discourse by giving us several parables as recorded in Matthew 24 and 25. These parables tell us how to live and where to place our focus as the final days approach. The primary message from the parables consistently emphasized three main points - watchfulness, preparedness and faithfulness as we face the imminence of the Second Coming. Collectively, the parables from this end time discussion stressed the importance of each of these three ideas.

Watch

Just as the entire world witnessed the dramatic and unprecedented rebirth of the nation of Israel in 1948, we have also seen global events consolidate just as Ezekiel foretold: Russia is now locked into military arms trading and economic alliances with many of the various terrorist supporting countries in the Middle-East – all of whom are violently opposed to the very existence of Israel. We've seen the rise of China as a world power, just as the book of Revelation foretold. We've seen the technology of the Mark of the Beast develop; technology which will allow for fulfillment of Revelation 13:16-17. The formation of the European Union has created a geopolitical alignment of European countries that appears exactly like the original Roman Empire, just as Daniel predicted. There are ten countries aligned in such a way that they may quite possibly represent the "ten kings" which have been described in the books of Daniel and Revelation. We've seen the terrorists groups and rogue nations develop nuclear technology which, for the first time in history can fulfill many of the various judgments described in Revelation. We also have global availability of television and satellite technology which permits "real-time" news events to be seen throughout the world, making the fulfillment of the Two Witnesses possible (Revelation 11:1-12). The whole world will see these two witnesses for Christ (probably Moses and Elijah) appear during the Tribulation, then die, and three days later miraculously become resurrected. The entire world is currently focused on events in Israel and Jerusalem, exactly as described by the prophet Zechariah over 2,500 years ago. The book of Daniel has become "unsealed" in these final days, just as predicted in Daniel 12. The book of Revelation is now understood in a literal manner, as modern technology has progressed. These facts alone serve to indicate that we nearing the last days. Jesus clearly stated that once we see these events taking place, we should know that His return is very near; that He would be right at the door.

Jesus also gave us important signs for which to watch. He said there would be war and rumors of war. Who could argue that the twentieth century did not bring more deaths from warfare than any other century? Who could argue that the persistent rumors of war haven't steadily increased towards the end of the twentieth century and into the current century? The cold war represented a 40 year period of a "rumor" of war. We see the constant threat of China invading Taiwan, which could escalate into global warfare. We have witnessed the threat from North Korea – both from their use of newly acquired nuclear technology and the constant threat to invade South Korea. There are wars in many countries in Africa, with mass genocide in some regions. Nuclear technology has finally escaped the tight reign previously held by the U.S. and Russia, and rogue nations now possess this capability. The U.S. war on terrorism has dramatically changed the world, as we see daily threats of terrorist activities consuming the nightly news. The war in Iraq persistently threatens to escalate into a wider war, potentially involving many of the surrounding nations. The war in Afghanistan continues without apparent ending. There is the rumor of India and Pakistan engaging in open warfare, with the potential use of their nuclear arsenals. The rumor of Islamic extremists widening their war against Christians and Jews persists. There is the rumor of Israel attacking Iran's nuclear plant; Iran has threatened wide-scale retaliation if this takes place. Rumors of war make news headlines almost every day, like never before in history particularly on such a wide scale.

Jesus told us to watch for the presence of famine and pestilence in the latter days. Worldwide starvation has reached epic proportions over the last several decades, as refugees have been forced to flee from numerous conflicts including Bosnia, Sudan, Ethiopia, Croatia, Afghanistan and Iraq. More face famine from world drought or flooding. The number of deaths from AIDS has increased steadily despite improvements in treatment modalities and treatment resistance is a growing concern. Tuberculosis has made a comeback. Polio is again making its appearance in many countries of the world. We see hospital acquired infections that are completely resistant to antibiotics surge in numbers. The deadly Ebola virus has not been contained as originally hoped.

Jesus mentioned earthquakes as a sign of the end times as well, and certainly one can easily obtain data which reveal the analogy to birth pains, as the quakes have peaked during four eras during the twentieth century. The 1990's have seen four separate years where the century average has been exceeded, 1992, 1995, 1996 and 1999. Jesus also said that there would be an increase in false teachings and apostasy in the Church at the same time as the other array of events – and undoubtedly the last few years have ushered in a time of religious leaders questioning the deity of Christ and His teachings. There are pastors and other Church leaders denying that Christ is God. Similarly, Christian persecution worldwide has dramatically increased and even in the U.S. we can see the very beginnings of overt Christian persecution. Currently, world-wide estimates reveal that over 150,000 Christians are killed annually for their beliefs – a number which far exceeds the entire number deaths from Roman persecution which took place over a 300 year period.

Each and every sign that we have been given, all pointing to the return of Christ, is now present. The number of significant prophetic events that have unfolded over the last 50 years is staggering. Prophetic events, just in the few brief years of the new century have been occurring at breathtaking speed. Either all of these factors taken together represent a massive coincidence, or we are indeed living in the last generation as described by Jesus. There is no mention in the Bible of a deceptive coincidence occurring in any generation. Therefore one must seriously consider all of these signs, as given by Jesus and the prophets, as real and applicable information directed to today's generation.

Prepare by Faith

Jesus told us with great emphasis to watch and prepare for His return. As Peter informed us, God does not desire that anyone perish; "He is patient with you, not wanting anyone to perish, but everyone to come to repentance." This is where the role of prophecy becomes clear. The scriptures make it vastly apparent that the last generation should know and understand that they are in fact, living in the final days. The reasons are also clear; we need to "prepare" by focusing on our faith and to watch for His return. We follow these instructions with great anticipation and hope because each prophetic event brings us closer and closer to eternity. The knowledge that Jesus is returning soon will allow us to serve as powerful witnesses during this final chapter of history. Because time is short, we need to inform as many people as possible of these truths.

God has given every individual free will. Each of us can decide exactly what our eternal fate will be. We can accept the gift of salvation simply by accepting Jesus Christ as our personal Lord and Savior, or we can reject that gift. By accepting this gift, we ensure what Jesus desperately wants: eternal life with each of His followers. By denial of this gift, and by rejecting Christ, we also determine our fate - eternity spent in the absence of God and the absence of His Kingdom.

Simply put, one can decide to either accept that the Bible contains these truths or one can reject the teachings in the Bible. Either Christ is wrong, or you are wrong. Jesus did not leave the possibility that he is simply a "great scholar" or just a "prophet". Jesus clearly stated that He is God, and that He is the only way to salvation. The Gospel of John makes this point abundantly clear.

Therefore, only three options exist with which to view Jesus: 1) He was a liar, 2) He was delusional and/or psychotic during His time on earth or, 3) He is God, who came to earth in human form. That's it. There are simply no other options regarding Christ, based upon everything He said and did. **Jesus did not allow for the popular opinion that He was simply a "great teacher" or a "good man", or even a "great philosopher".** If the first option above is true, then He was not a great teacher, nor was He a prophet, as both scenarios are inconsistent with being a liar. If the second option is true, then again, He could not have been a great philosopher/teacher because this scenario is inconsistent with psychosis. Additionally, over a three year period it is hard to imagine that overt psychosis would not have been recognized by the followers of Christ. As a Physician reviewing His teachings, there is absolutely no evidence that He was mentally unstable in any way. His thoughts and teachings were amazingly complex and coherent. It is also hard to imagine that a group of apostles and disciples would follow someone with overt psychosis or a pathological liar, for a three year period, and then subsequently die horrible deaths in support of such a person.

The most appropriate conclusion based upon eyewitness evidence, documentary evidence, corroborating evidence, scientific evidence, medical evidence and circumstantial evidence is that Jesus Christ is who He said: One and the same as God, who willingly died on the cross for the singular purpose of man's salvation (1, 2, 3). There is a massive amount of evidence that God exists as the creator and there is an equal amount of "data" confirming that Jesus was exactly who He said He is. The clear, unambiguous message from the Bible is that our personal relationship with Jesus Christ and acceptance of these facts will determine our eternal destiny.

At the time of Jesus' death the apostles were hiding in fear. Peter even denied that he knew Christ on three separate occasions because of this fear. Yet suddenly, beginning only three days after His death, the followers of Jesus were publically proclaiming the Gospel and they were willing to be persecuted and even put to gruesome deaths for their belief. What changed? I don't know anyone who is willing to die for a lie. The followers of Christ did not die for what they believed; they died for what they had *seen*, as written in 2 Peter 1:16:

> "We did not follow cleverly invented stories when we told you about the power and coming of our Lord Jesus Christ, but we were eyewitnesses of his majesty."

They *saw* a resurrected Jesus Christ – that is the single factor that changed over this three day period.

Sadly, most of the people I know who have not accepted the gift of salvation remain completely ignorant of the Bible and the overwhelming evidence of data which support the truths described. There are volumes of books and scientific literature which give tangible "data" to support the existence of Jesus exactly as described in the Bible – yet many never bother to research these facts. Many folks declare that they don't have the time to research these issues, nor have they considered the issue of their eternal fate. I find that many people spend far more time researching what type of car to buy, or where to take their next vacation, rather than researching the issue of their eternity, and the fate of their souls. In other cases, it seems that people are afraid of what acceptance of biblical truths could do to their lives – in other words, they *will not* consider these truths, as they might have to abandon their previously held beliefs or perhaps even abandon their way of life. That thought is overwhelming to some. Still others have a fear of social rejection – they feel that their peer groups might reject them or ridicule them if they seriously consider the truths written in the Bible.

Many people simply feel that if they live a "good life" or if they are a "good person" then they will reach heaven – after all "good people" get to heaven don't they? The vast majority of people consider that we all have souls which will exist for eternity. Unfortunately, many agree with the premise that simply being "good" is the requirement for eternal life in the heavenly realm. However, such a premise makes no sense, nor does it point to a loving, fair God. The problem with this approach is that no one can define what being "good" really means. No religion, including Christianity can define exactly what these good works would be – certainly no definition exists which would enable one to follow these "rules" of works in a specific manner. Even the Ten Commandments given in the Bible have absolutely no link to one's salvation. So how "good" is good enough? Shouldn't God at least define this?

Most people have never tested this assumption that "good people" go to heaven. Under this scenario, unlike popular opinion, God would neither be fair nor loving. If, for instance, God did allow people to enter heaven based on being "good", then why doesn't He at least define what being "good" involves? Why would He make us guess what this means? Andy Stanley, in his excellent book "How Good is Good Enough?" gives great detail to these issues (4) and asks the following questions:

> "If there is a level of performance that will get us into heaven and God neglects to tell us exactly what it is, can we with good conscience call Him good? As an employer, you wouldn't withhold a job description from your employees and then evaluate them by a standard they never had an opportunity to see. As a teacher you wouldn't give tests on material you never covered. When mere mortals act in this manner, we complain vehemently. We yank our kids out of these

schools. We refuse to work for those kinds of
companies. We expect more from our fellow
man. Yet when it comes to God, somehow
we have grown accustomed to his duplicity.
Apparently the whole world had."

What if this standard of "good" was somehow reduced
to mathematical terms – something we can all understand.
Under this scenario, let's assume that we needed for 80% of
our lives to be engaged in "good works" in order to gain
entry into heaven. What about the "good" person who
achieved only 79% of "good works" and thus barely came
up short? Is this scenario fair? Probably not if you were that
person who was only 1% from reaching heaven. Maybe if
he/she had just known that they were only 1% short they
could have done a few extra good acts – or if they had just
had one more day on earth to get that extra 1% - then all
would have been fine. That person simply ran out of time.
Does this seem fair? This is not a silly question, because if
you truly believe in "works" based judgment, then these are
the obvious questions.

What about a persons "internal" sense of right and
wrong? Shouldn't that serve as the basis of being good
enough to reach heaven? The problem with this approach is
obvious – everyone would have a different standard of judgment. How fair is this approach? In addition, we know that
our concept of "good" changes over the years. Most people
have very different concepts of "good" versus "bad"
through their aging process, as do different cultures and religions. So which life era would God choose for the judgment? When we were in our 20's? 30's? Retirement age?
Shouldn't this be included in the information that we need
to know for our "works based" salvation? Yet mysteriously,
God hides all of this vital information.

Perhaps more importantly in this discussion, is the fact

that notion of being "good" or doing good "works" in order to reach heaven is contradictory to the teachings of Jesus. The teachings of Jesus are the exact opposite of what most people in the world believe. In fact, Jesus taught that good people don't necessarily go to heaven. According to Jesus, only *forgiven* people go to heaven, and this forgiveness is made possible by the sacrificial death of Jesus Christ. An honest assessment of this "system" reveals the magnificence of this plan. The real reason "good" people don't go to heaven is because there aren't any good people – we are all sinners. In God's eyes, none of us have purity or holiness which is necessary to stand in the presence of God in heaven.

Jesus proved this point once and for all during His last minutes on the cross, as He approached death along with two other criminals. He proved on the cross that works do not set the standard for acceptance into God's Kingdom – only belief in Christ and His forgiveness and mercy. The scene on the cross gives a beautiful example of this fact. One of the criminals admitted that he was receiving his just punishment; however he opened his heart to Jesus just before his death:

> "We are punished justly, for we are getting what our deeds deserve. But this man has done nothing wrong. Then he said, 'Jesus, remember me when you come into your kingdom'. Jesus answered him, 'I tell you the truth, today you will be with me in paradise.'"

Not only had this criminal failed to engage in "good works", but according to his own words, he deserved this extreme punishment because of his "bad works". Clearly this was not someone who would traditionally fall into the category of "saved" – yet that is exactly what Jesus did for him as he hung on the cross dying.

Because God is perfect, holy and absolute, He simply cannot be in the presence of sin. He is incompatible with sin in every way. For this reason, there is only one way to reconcile ourselves to God, as we all fall short of the perfection required to be in God's presence. The true and only path to salvation according to the teachings of the Bible is repentance of our sins and placing our total faith in Christ's sacrificial death on the cross. John 3:16-18 clarifies:

> *"For God so loved the world that he gave his one and only Son, that whoever believes in him shall not perish but have eternal life. For God did not send his Son into the world to condemn the world, but to save the world through him. Whoever believes in him is not condemned, but whoever does not believe stands condemned already because he has not believed in the name of God's one and only Son."*

Each individual on earth has rebelled against God through our sins. Romans 3:22 tells us that we therefore require righteousness from God which only comes through faith in Jesus Christ. Romans 3:23 explains the following, *"for all have sinned and fall short of the glory of God, and are justified freely by his grace through the redemption that came by Christ Jesus."*

The scriptures explain that our sinful rebellion has removed us from the holiness of God and subsequently prevents us from entering heaven unless our sins are forgiven and we are made pure. Romans 6:23 declares the following: *"For the wages of sin is death, but the gift of God is eternal life in Christ Jesus our Lord."*

This gift which Jesus made possible on the cross and by His resurrection, gives all humans something very special.

It's something that requires no work on our part - that work was done on the cross. We don't have to earn it. Jesus did all of the work by His sinless life on earth and His death on the cross. Once we accept this gift, our eternal destiny is sealed. We will spend eternity in a place that Jesus is preparing specifically for each one of us. A place which is so grand and magnificent that we cannot even imagine it – even in our wildest fantasies. All we have to do is to simply accept this gift. The choice is ours.

The Search for Truth

You may or may not believe in these statements at this time in your life. Perhaps you have been interested in prophecy but you are not as interested in matters involving salvation or eternal destiny. Perhaps you have struggled with believing that the Bible is indeed the true words from God, or perhaps it's all just too overwhelming to consider. Maybe you have heard the various bits of folklore and myths involving the Bible that make it difficult to believe. Maybe you simply don't like the Christians next door or maybe you have had bad experiences with the Church. Perhaps you simply haven't had the time to explore one way or the other because of ongoing daily demands.

If any of these descriptions are true or if similar ideas have been keeping you from exploring the issue of your eternal destiny I would urge you to spend at least a reasonable amount of time searching for the truth. The stakes are high – this is by far the biggest decision one will ever face. Even if you have chosen to not believe in any God, then you have still made a choice. My hope is that whatever choice you eventually make, for something as important as eternal destiny, will be based upon well-researched and well-considered information. We don't usually make important choices in life based on things such as myth, folklore, rumor, innuendo, social status, or even small fragments of information – yet this is how many well-educated, intelligent people determine their ultimate fate.

The references given at the end of this chapter may appeal to the scientific mind in terms of the presenting the vast amount of information available regarding the Bible, the life, death and resurrection of Jesus and much of the documented "evidence" that I believe God has provided for those seeking the truth. The body of evidence supporting these truths is remarkable and to an objective mind, unequivocal. Despite the array of available evidence however, one must ultimately ask the following question: "Is Jesus who he claimed to be?" According to Jesus himself the answer is clear: *"I am the resurrection and the life. He who believes in me will live, even though he dies; and whoever lives and believes in me will never die. Do you believe this?"* (John 11:2).

From the evidence presented in this book, it appears that we are indeed living at the end of this current age. World events are moving rapidly towards a final climax; a time of tribulation that has never before been experienced on earth. The ancient prophets gave us multiple signs - signs that would be witnessed by the final generation, intended to serve as warning signals that the end is approaching. Objective analyses of the scriptures confirm the fact that virtually all remaining prophecies are unfolding during the present era. For this reason, we should do as Jesus suggested in His parables – to be prepared, faithful and watching for His return. As Jesus discussed His Second Coming, He informed the disciples of a profound truth (Luke 21:28):

> *"When these things begin to take place, stand up and lift up your heads, because your redemption is drawing near."*

CHAPTER TWELVE NOTES

1. Lee Strobel. The Case for Christ. A Journalist's Personal Investigation of the Evidence for Jesus (Zondervan Publishing House. 1998).

2. Lee Strobel. A Case for a Creator. A Journalist Investigates Scientific Evidence that Points Toward God (Zondervan Publishing House. 2004).

3. Grant R. Jeffrey. The Signature of God. Documented Evidence That Proves Beyond Doubt the Bible is the Inspired Word of God (W Publishing Group – Thomas Nelson Inc. 1998).

4. Andy Stanley. How Good is Good Enough? (Multnomah Publishers, Inc.).

Printed in the United States
36601LVS00002B/25-54